THE SOMERSET CRICKET QUIZ BOOK

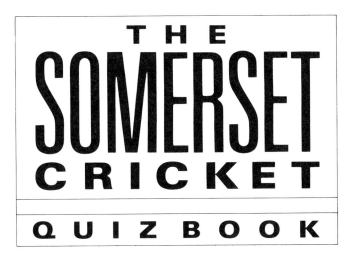

THE SOMERSET CRICKET QUIZ BOOK

BOB CRAMPSEY

MAINSTREAM
PUBLISHING

First published in Great Britain in 1988 by
MAINSTREAM PUBLISHING COMPANY (EDINBURGH) LTD.
7 Albany Street
Edinburgh EH1 3UG

ISBN 1 85158 121 9 (paper)

British Library Cataloguing in Publication Data:

Crampsey, Robert A. (Robert Anthony), *1930-*
    Somerset cricket quiz book.
    1. Somerset. County cricket. Clubs:
    Somerset County Cricket Club, to 1983
    I. Title
    796.35'863'094238

ISBN 1-85158-121-9

Typeset in Times by Pulse Origination, Edinburgh.
Printed in Great Britain by Butler & Tanner Ltd, Frome, Somerset.

Contents

SOMERSET CRICKET
— A Love Affair For Life

Following Somerset cricket is not a pastime or a hobby, it is a disease from which death supplies the only release. It is totally irrational, how else explain the fact that I, a Scot, never domiciled nearer Somerset than 400 miles distance, should be so besotted with this most euphonious-sounding of counties? Nor can I claim the normal sporting wish to be associated with success. When I first took a lively and abiding interest in Somerset they were propping up the county championship for four years in succession. Even in their recent years of comparative affluence, most summers ended for me in a blaze of fury as I drove back to Scotland having seen some Championship match tossed away from an apparently assured position of victory.

Thus a first-innings lead of 200 at Old Trafford with a stupendous 130 plus from Ian Botham in an hour and a half was followed by the loss of the match which an old Somerset hand should have anticipated. We were much more likely to have won had we trailed at the halfway stage by the same margin.

For well over a century, even the county's survival has seemed improbable most of the time. Comparatively small, agricultural, with no great centres of population, it has always had to rely very heavily on imported players. Perhaps it has over-relied on them for in the darkest days of the 1950s there were seasons in which as few as two Somerset-born players took the field whereas in the halcyon times of 1979-82 there were frequently as many as six native sons in the side. There were quite a few good players within the county boundary — there still are — and players are emerging now that time and money is being expended in their recruitment.

More than any other county, perhaps, Somerset has marched to a different drum. They are one of a melancholy band of three which has never won the county championship and, until very recently, prevailing attitudes within the club made it extremely unlikely that they ever would do so. The committee's admirable if belated stand of 1986 makes the championship pennant much more a possibility — some day.

Somerset were the last upholders of the amateur approach to cricket, and the word could be used in both its pejorative and complimentary sense where the county was concerned. For the first eighty years of its existence the influence of the amateur was paramount and indeed Somerset would not take the field regularly with a majority of professionals until the 1950s.

There were great amateur players, the Palairets, Sammy Woods, Jack White, all of whom were available on a regular basis. There were the great proconsuls of empire such as W. F. T. Greswell and M. D. Lyon who would emerge every fifth year from Ceylon or Africa to brighten the summer of their long leaves with top-class displays. T. C. Lowry was smuggled in from the Wellington of the Antipodes and social cricketers such as R. C. Robertson-Glasgow became much more than that with constant exposure to the county game.

Since the Guy Earles and C. C. C. Cases of the world did not depend on the game for a living, they were able to play in the style which came naturally to them and that was a cavalier approach which did not believe that any bowler was good enough to tie them down. He might be good enough to get them out but not to tie them down. Even in the 1930s R. A. Ingle and R. J. O. Meyer could take time off from the law and school-mastering to skipper the county side.

All that is not to lose sight of the fact that Somerset had always been constrained to field amateurs who were not even of good club standard and whose major recommendations were that they were there and possessed of motor cars which they would put at the disposal of the club. In the grim post-war years there was no long-term future for the genuine amateur. The Denis Silks and the Colin Atkinsons could spare a couple of years perhaps to captain but the commitment of such a fine player as Micky Walford, arguably the best Somerset amateur batsman of the twentieth century, could be measured in weeks rather than seasons.

By the late 1950s the hopeless task of finding an amateur captain had been abandoned. The leadership of Somerset has been one of the most interesting strands in the texture of the county's history. There have been the great skippers, H. T. Hewett, Sammy Woods, John Daniell, Jack White and, much more recently, Brian Close. There have been the very good captains, Bunty Longrigg, Colin Atkinson, Peter Roebuck, whose work in the face of a difficult inheritance has been totally admirable and, before him, Brian Rose. There have been those who conceived it to be their duty to serve but found the task uncongenial. I would identify Brian Langford and Roy Kerslake in that category, while the occasional appointment, such as those of Ben Brocklehurst and Ian Botham has been disastrous, and in the latter case deeply damaging. Maurice Tremlett and Harold Stephenson, more than any others, deserve the credit of restoring credibility to a side that had become a byword as a good-natured shambles.

And what of the professionals? Only a handful of them in the early days, Braund, Robson, Tyler, Nichols, and not even dignified with initials or first name in the rigid caste system of the time. For 70 years the professionals carried the bowling load because although White, Robertson-Glasgow and Sammy Woods all bowled they were the exceptions, amateurs batted and professionals bowled. Between the wars Gimblett (whose dislike of amateurs bordered on the irrational), the Lee brothers, Jack and Frank, Arthur Wellard and Bertie Buse provided with Wally Luckes the nucleus round which the glittering array of fancy blazers came and went.

There were the great players and the great servants, not always inhabiting the same body. Harold Gimblett was marvellous value for the pittance he was paid, mainly because he doesn't appear to have liked Test cricket very much and, even if he had, he was playing in the days before its appalling expansion. Both Wellard and Andrews were two cricketers for the price of one and Maurice Tremlett, nagged at to change a perfectly serviceable bowling action, survived its total disappearance to become one of the finest county batsmen of his day.

In the 1950s and 1960s Somerset were a highly unfashionable county and, but for this, players such as Graham Atkinson and Roy Virgin of the batsmen, Brian Langford as a spinner and Harold Stephenson behind the stumps must have been asked to play for England. Ken Palmer too, as a fine all-rounder, would have received more than the single fiddler's bidding he was given to join the England side.

Increasingly in the last 30 years there has been an irreconcilable conflict between the calls of country and county. The award of an England cap means that in many cases the county might just as well forget about the player concerned. His availability is greatly restricted and even when there his commitment is all too often lacking. This is not a problem exclusive to Somerset, Sussex had it with John Snow and Warwickshire with Bob Willis.

In the case of Somerset, the threat was three-fold. Ian Botham is undoubtedly the greatest natural talent ever to have graced the club, but the huge bulk of his contribution to it occurred before his England call-up or, at best, in the four years immediately following it. There were still occasional performances which would have been quite beyond anyone else but they became more and more rare in the three-day matches which are the heart of the first-class world. Those who attended Somerset matches were conscious of the keen irony whereby the world's leading Test wicket-taker had become almost a joke bowler on the county circuit.

All this is just as likely to be the fault of the lunatic international schedule of the 1980s as of the player. Joel Garner, too, evidently found the demands of the championship game excessive, but the championship nevertheless accounts for two-thirds of the season. And it was also noticeable that Viv Richards, every bit as great a Test player, was much more often capable of performing at his brilliant best than the other two. He missed more matches than in his early seasons, granted, but his influence on the ones he played was immense. For a decade he has been the greatest batsman in the world at Test *and* county level.

This book is in its way a history of the club and therefore contains, and rightly contains, much about the day-to-day players who make triumphs possible. Names such as Peter Denning, Derek Taylor, Vic Marks, Colin Dredge all appear frequently and so they should. They are only lesser players in the judgement, sometimes flawed, of the selectors and their contribution to the success of their side has been immense, to say nothing of the pleasure they have given on their own and visiting grounds.

Even in the grudging days of the 1980s it behoves us to remember opponents and praise them where they have earned praise. Hobbs, Woolley, Hutton, Compton, Grace, Jessop, Fry, Ranji, Sobers, Bradman, Sutcliffe, in no particular order these great players have honoured the Somerset grounds and in the more relaxed dispensation of modern times we have been able to claim such as Sunil Gavaskar, Steve Waugh and Martin Crowe as our own, for a time at least.

The county championship is the lynch-pin of the first-class game and must remain so but it would be foolish and distorting to ignore the arrival of the one-day match, the more so in that it has exclusively provided the club's successes to date. It has brought several new skills to cricket and a new type of crowd. This last is all too frequently raucous and foul-mouthed but I have the notion that it may more nearly approach the crowds of the late eighteenth-century matches of Lord Frederick Beauclerk and his friends than the douce and decorous three-day assemblies.

As the first-class game has become more commercialised — and it had to so become — fixtures have tended to fall back on the county grounds throughout the country and the outlying small venues have largely disappeared. Frome, Yeovil, Wells, Glastonbury, Street — Somerset have been particularly hard hit — but they are all to be found in these pages for each and every one stamped its mark on Somerset cricket.

They are all part and parcel of Somerset cricket, the old, decrepit but ineffably aristocratic pavilion at Taunton which even yet makes its successor across the ground seem a bit of a *parvenu,* the doll's house pavilions at Bath and Weston and the grey, almost black sight-screens at the latter, an argument for the white ball if ever there was one.

The umpires who gave the decisions, the players who accepted them with good or ill grace, they are all here. The players who could not play often enough, the players who should never have been allowed near a county side and yet who in some strange way enriched the game by being so, they are all here. The improbable victories, snatched from the jaws of defeat. The infinitely more numerous and even more improbable defeats snatched from the jaws of victory, they too are here.

Questions and answers are about facts, opinions must be left to the reader but the author may be allowed a few final impressions. In my ideal match it is always the five-minute bell before the start of play at Bath or Weston (rarely Taunton). With the customary freedom accorded the writer I am about to see *all* the things which have made Somerset such a marvellous part of my life. I will see Denning and Rose run between the wickets, no two ever ran the short single more swiftly or more safely. Richards will take his supple stroll to the wicket at number four. I will want Roebuck somewhere in the first five. He has the gift of concentration given to very few Somerset players. Bill Alley to bowl medium pace, that's certain, with the youthful Joel to open. I would send one of the players off quite deliberately so that I might once more have the pleasure of seeing Hallam Moseley (who might otherwise not make this team) throw from the boundary with his flat, low trajectory.

Botham to hit (was there ever a ferocious hitter whose bat was straighter?) and Derek Taylor and Harold Stephenson to keep at alternate ends. I once saw Stephenson stump his Glamorgan opposite number at Bath, off Palmer I think. Three of us, directly behind the bowler's arm and all experienced scorers, were in the process of recording the wicket as bowled when we saw the square-leg umpire confirming the decision to an equally astonished score-box. The movement of the hands had not even been a blur.

Who else? I'd have Brian Close calling the shots and the field-placings, even if from a deckchair in front of the Bath pavilion and no matter how many I've already mentioned (and you will remember I have artistic licence) I would have Colin Dredge because he stands for eternal Somerset values, indeed eternal cricketing values. I'd include Phil Slocombe and Jeremy Lloyds, two who got away and were given less than a fair chance, perhaps, to show that committees are fallible, and I must have Martin Crowe as a token of hope for our future.

I see what I have done very clearly. My match will end up as Somerset A v. Somerset B, and why shouldn't it? Well, then, my last six (remember Ken Palmer is there) will be those whom I did not see but dearly wish I had. It would be criminal not to pick Lionel Palairet and the great Corinthian Sammy Woods. John Daniell, not so much as a player as a thank you for keeping the club in being and John Cornish White, farmer and spinner extraordinary. Harold Gimblett whom I just missed and Micky Walford, whom I just caught. I would like to see them open in a long partnership to compare notes.

You'll allow me two twelfth men. I'd take Bertie Buse for the same reasons I took Colin Dredge and R. J. O. Meyer, "Boss" Meyer, to represent the streak of eccentricity that the club has worn as a badge of honour.

The sides are out; I'll leave you to the questions. They span 112 years. Some of them you will find much too easy. Others — well . . . .. All, I hope, will prove stimulating and of some interest.

Questions

CAPTAINS COURAGEOUS

1 Which Somerset captain had the initials S. M. J.?
2 Which Somerset skipper was known as "The Prophet"?
3 Which two Somerset captains have been headmasters of Millfield School?
4 Which Somerset captain was a Berkshire farmer?
5 Which Somerset captain was a Somerset farmer?
6 Which Somerset captain was born on a Red Indian reservation?
7 Which Somerset captain was a serving naval officer?
8 Which three players shared the captaincy officially in 1948?
9 Which Somerset captain was known as "Bunty"?
10 Which Somerset captain did the double in his first season in county cricket?

COUNTY GROUNDS

11 On what ground did Harold Gimblett hit the fastest century of the first-class season of 1935 on his debut for Somerset?
12 On what ground did Arthur Wellard hit five sixes in one over v. Derbyshire in 1936?
13 Name two grounds on which Somerset have played at Yeovil.
14 And the ground at Bristol.
15 Which distinguished Somerset John Player League bowling performance was given at Glastonbury by Graham Burgess?
16 What is the name of the county ground at Bath?
17 On which ground outside the county did Somerset first play in the John Player League?
18 Where did the inaugural meeting of Somerset County Cricket Club decide that the county ground should be?
19 What rivers flow past the grounds at Bath and Taunton?
20 To which player is the Memorial Gates at the County Ground, Taunton, dedicated?

THE COUNTY CHAMPIONSHIP

21 What was unusual about the county championship matches of 1919?

22 And those of 1939?

23 When did Somerset tie a game because the last opposing batsman took more than two minutes to arrive at the wicket?

24 Who beat Somerset in a day in 1947?

25 Who did likewise in 1953?

26 Who was the last Somerset player to do the double?

27 How many players have kept wicket for England and Somerset since the Second World War?

28 How many championship centuries did Bill Alley score when making his 3000 runs in 1961?

29 Which batsman scored three centuries against Northants between the years 1982 and 1983?

30 What is the highest score by a Somerset player in the county championship?

JOHN PLAYER LEAGUE

31 On which ground did Somerset win the John Player League title of 1979?

32 On which ground did Norman McVicker hit the last two balls for sixes to win the game for Leicestershire?

33 Who was the unfortunate bowler?

34 A Somerset bowler holds an unsurpassable record in Sunday League cricket. Who is he?

35 Trevor Gard had two serious injuries while keeping wicket in John Player League matches for Somerset. Who took over behind the stumps in the matches affected?

36 Name the fast bowler who returned a fine analysis at Bath in a J.P.L. match against Lancashire in 1980 while deputising for Joel Garner.

37 What noteworthy performance did Bob Clapp record in the J.P.L.?

38 What is the most northerly ground on which Somerset have played in the Sunday league?

39 What is Joel Garner's best bowling performance v. Gloucestershire?

40 And Ian Botham's best batting performance in the Sunday game?

41 Identify the following amateurs from their initials (a) M. M. (b) G. R. S. (c) H. H.
42 And these (a) A. A. (b) C. C. C. (c) L. St. V.
43 Name the Somerset amateur who played *for* the West Indies *against* England before the Second World War.
44 Name the four Somerset players who played for the Gentlemen against Players in 1924.
45 Who was the prominent Somerset amateur cricketer who was killed in the Second World War?
46 Who was the amateur captain who scored 1000 runs for Somerset in 1950?
47 Who was the England rugby full-back who played a trial for Somerset in the match in which A. C. McLaren made 424 for Lancashire at Taunton?
48 Who was Somerset's first captain in first-class cricket?
49 Lionel Palairet was one of the great Somerset amateur batsman. Who was the brother who later became club president?
50 Name the amateur who scored four centuries in three matches in 1908.

Which Somerset players were known as

51 Crusoe?
52 Dasher?
53 Budgie?
54 The Demon of Frome?
55 The Big Bird?
56 The Farmer?
57 Sammy?
58 Dar?
59 Chico?
60 Sir Len?

61 When Bill Alley made 3019 runs in 1961 how many centuries did he make all told?

62 How many wickets did he take in that season?

63 What was his record in Australia as a professional boxer?

64 What record did he set in the match against Surrey at Taunton in June 1961?

65 How many runs did he score that year in the match at Taunton against the touring Australian side?

66 How many centuries did he hit for Somerset in that season?

67 How many other first-class players have made ten centuries in a season at the age of 42?

68 What was his lowest match aggregate in that season?

69 Alley was one of two Somerset players picked to play against the Gentlemen that year. Who was the other?

70 How many balls did Bill Alley bowl against Essex at Yeovil in 1960 without conceding a run?

MORE NICKNAMES

Which Somerset players answer or answered to the following nicknames

71 Mandy?

72 Babe?

73 Chimp?

74 Rupert?

75 Twitch?

A VARSITY MATCH

76 What was unusual about the match between Somerset and Cambridge University at Taunton in 1960.

77 Name the Cambridge bat who scored a century in each innings.

78 Name the Somerset cricketer who failed by one run to match this feat.

79 Name the other two Somerset players who made centuries in this game.
80 Name the TV commentator who had a first-innings century for Cambridge.

JOHN CORNISH WHITE

81 What was the combined playing span of J. C. White and Lionel Palairet?
82 Against which county did J. C. White take ten for 16 in 1921 and 16 wickets in 1919?
83 How often did J. C. White score 1000 runs in a season?
84 Jack White holds the Somerset record for catches. How many?

OVERSEAS ALLEGIANCES

The following Somerset players appeared with states, provinces or districts abroad. Identify their overseas sides.

85 D. J. S. Taylor in South Africa.
86 Vic Marks in Australia.
87 Martin Crowe in New Zealand.
88 Viv Richards in the West Indies.

R. C. ROBERTSON-GLASGOW

89 What did R. C. stand for?
90 Which public school did he attend?
91 How many appearances did he make for Oxford in the Varsity match?
92 What was his career span with Somerset?
93 What was his best bowling performance for them?
94 Who nicknamed him Robinson Crusoe?
95 He shared in only two century partnerships, each time with the same batsman. Who was the other person?

WHOSE BENEFIT?

96 Who ruined his own benefit match against Somerset?

97 How did he do this?

98 For what other feat was he noted?

ARTHUR WELLARD

99 How long did Wellard play with Somerset?

100 Twice he hit five sixes in an over. One of the bowlers to suffer was Armstrong of Derbyshire. Who was the other?

101 What advice was he repeatedly given when he unsuccessfully asked his native county, Kent, for a trial?

102 He was selected to go on the England tour which had to be cancelled because of the outbreak of war in 1939. Where would this tour have been going?

103 Who was the Australian bowler whom he hit onto the grandstand balcony during the Lord's Test of 1938?

JACK WHITE

104 What was White's "Miracle of Brisbane"?

105 On that tour in 1928 he was vice-captain. Who was the captain?

106 White took over in 1928 as captain for the last Test, a game which set a record. Why?

107 What was his performance in the Adelaide Test of that series?

108 What were his batting and bowling aggregates for Somerset?

NICKNAMES AND TERMS OF ABUSE

In recent Somerset dressing-rooms who answers or answered to the following terms of endearment?

109 Pacman?

110 Pooch?

111 Jo'burg?

112 Ghostie?

113 Pedlar?

114 Rosie?

115 Harry?

116 Ziggy?

117 Earp?

118 Twiglets?

FOR AND AGAINST

119 Which Somerset player has a father who was both captain and president of Somerset?

120 Which Somerset batsman scored 174 for Cambridge in the Varsity match of 1986?

121 Which recently retired cricketer had his career-best bowling figures against Somerset at Bristol in 1986?

122 Who was the first Somerset player since Harold Gimblett to score a first-class century on his debut?

123 At Headingly in 1985 "Mutley" scored a career-best 90 for Yorkshire against Somerset. What is "Mutley's" real name?

THE UMPIRES LIST OF 1987

124 Name the two umpires on the 1987 list who played for Somerset when under 17 years of age?

125 Which umpire was educated at Taunton School but never played for Somerset?

126 Who is the umpire who played for Somerset and whose nickname is "Buckets"?

127 Which umpire has a one in four chance of standing in a match where one of his former teams is involved?

128 Which umpire attended Backwell Secondary Modern School in Nailsea?

129 Can you name the two brothers on the umpires list in 1987?

130 Did they have anything else in common?

131 Which of them was born within the county?

132 In what country did Ken Palmer play his only Test match?

133 Who is the senior umpire on the panel?

134 When was he first appointed?

135 How many brothers did he have and how many were Test cricketers?

THE YEAR 1966

136 What was unusual about the championship matches of 1966?

137 In this season Somerset first played competitive Sunday cricket. Where and against whom?

138 Who was the bowler who returned figures against Notts. at Trent Bridge 17.2–14–10–7?

139 What significance did the match against Glamorgan at Cardiff on August 13, 1966, have?

140 What record did Roy Virgin set during the season?

HARD-LUCK STORIES

141 Who was the amateur who in his first season and at the age of 19 took 76 wickets but could never play regularly because he became a tea-planter in Ceylon?

142 Who was the Somerset batsman who was picked for England, never got an innings and was never selected again for a Test?

143 Which Somerset cricketer spent much of World War One as an interned prisoner of war in Holland?

144 If Arthur Wellard had played for his native county which badge would have been on his cap?

PETER WIGHT

145 What was Peter Wight's highest career score?

146 Peter Wight set up a new record aggregate of 2316 runs in the season of 1960. Who had previously held it?

147 How long did Peter Wight's record last?

148 Where was Peter Wight's birthplace?

149 What did he have in common with Bill Alley after retiral?

150 Who was the first Somerset player to score 1000 runs for the county in the year of his first-class debut?

151 Which Somerset cricketer was one of Wisden's Five Players of the Year in 1971?

152 Who was the Somerset bowler who returned Gillette Cup figures of 12–4–15–1 against Northumberland in 1977?

153 Who were the two batsmen who put on 251 against Surrey at Weston in 1977 for the fourth wicket?

154 Who went for 74 in eight overs (taking one wicket) against Kent in the John Player League in 1970 at Weston (Devonshire Road)?

COUNTY CHAMPIONSHIPS

155 Which county has beaten Somerset on four occasions within a day in County championship matches?

156 What was unusual about the playing hours for county championship matches in the 1968 season?

157 What is the minimum number of championship matches scheduled in a season for Somerset since 1946?

158 And the maximum?

159 In which season did Somerset go through the championship unbeaten until the last match?

TESTERS

160 Name two New Zealand Test players who have played for Somerset.

161 And two Indian Test players.

162 Four Australian Test players who have done likewise.

163 One of the Somerset players: N. S. Mitchell-Innes, M. Tremlett, H. W. Stephenson, K. Palmer is not a Test cricketer. Which one?

164 Has Somerset ever staged an international match?

165 Which Minor County did Somerset lose to in the Nat. West competition of 1987?

166 Who was the player who fell four runs short of making a double century in consecutive visits to Bath?

167 Who were the two Middlesex batsmen who had a stand of 424 against Somerset at Lord's in 1948?

168 In season 1987 a player scored a century and took twelve wickets in the same match against Somerset. Who was he?

169 What is the highest individual score recorded against Somerset?

170 For which Minor County did Harold Gimblett play?

171 Which trophy was he awarded for his century against Essex at Frome in 1935?

172 From which Test did he withdraw because of a carbuncle on his neck?

173 How did he spend his war service?

174 With which public school was he associated as coach and groundsman?

175 What was unusual about the fifth Test against the West Indies at Headingley in 1980 from the Somerset point of view?

176 Who was the Somerset player who became part of the first instance of brothers hitting a century in the same innings of a Test match?

177 Which player who was later to have a Somerset connection scored three centuries in three successive Tests in Australia in 1977-78?

178 Miles Coope and Johnny Lawrence both came from the same cricketing background. What was it?

179 Who was the Warwickshire bowler who did the hat-trick against Somerset at Taunton in May 1947?

180 The Somerset side of 1947 did the double against the champions. Who were the 1947 champions?

181 What was odd about the second innings bowling of Middlesex in the Taunton match that year?

182 In this match a Middlesex amateur got a century on his debut. Name?

183 Who scored a double century for Surrey at the Oval in July 1949? Two clues: an opener and left-handed.

184 What other Surrey player got a century in their 501 for three declared?

MISCELLANEOUS

185 What was noteworthy about A. D. E. Rippon's 119 against Essex at Leyton, 1919?

186 How many centuries did A. E. S. Rippon make for Somerset?

187 Who was the army officer who played very occasionally for Somerset but made 42 and 63 against Larwood at Taunton in 1928?

188 Who was the wicket-keeper who continued in club cricket until he was 80 and who had 416 victims for Somerset?

189 Who was the Somerset bowler who against Derbyshire at Frome in 1951 took seven for 23?

190 Name the Boer War soldier, later an Assistant District Commissioner in Southern Nigeria, who scored 122 out of 630 against Yorkshire at Leeds in 1901?

191 Who played for Middlesex and Surrey and later became Treasurer of the M.C.C. and President of Somerset?

192 On which Kent ground did J. R. Mason score 126 against Somerset and take 10 for 180 in 1904?

193 Who was the Test bowler who played chiefly for Surrey and London County but came to Somerset for a brief spell at the end of his illustrious career?

194 Who was the Yorkshire player who took Martin Crowe apart during a Sunday League match at Middlesbrough in 1984?

195 Who dismissed Jack Hobbs in the only match he himself played for Somerset?

196 Name the Surrey batsman, known as "The Guv'nor", who scored 357* against Somerset at The Oval in 1899?

197 What was the Surrey total in that match?

198 On which ground did Bill Alley score his 3000th run in September 1961?

199 Name the Keynsham batsman of the 1980s whose highest score for Somerset was 99*?

200 For what other sport is Clarence Park used?

201 And Bath?

202 For what other sport has the county ground at Taunton been used?

203 Can you name the Somerset skipper who was capped by Scotland in a Boys' International golf match?

204 Who was the John Player League record holder (first to 2000 runs and 200 wickets) who recorded his highest first-class score against Somerset?

205 He started his first-class career in the year when England won the soccer World Cup and he hit 227 for Northants against Somerset in 1976. Who is he and where was it?

206 What record did he set that day and who helped him to it?

207 What is Julian Wyatt's highest score in first-class cricket?

With which public schools do you connect the following Somerset players, either as pupils, teachers or coaches:

208 R. J. O. Meyer?

209 M. M. Walford?

210 Harold Gimblett?

211 H. Watts?

212 Colin Atkinson?

213 Denis Silk?

214 Why was M. M. Walford unavailable for selection by Somerset in the summer of 1950?

215 Who was the Somerset player whose father conducted the enquiry into public safety at Association Football grounds?

216 Who asked for "four more gerania, Crusoe", and why?

217 In the Gillette Cup of 1965 against Berkshire one of the Minor County's players was Man of the Match. Which one?

218 Who was the Scottish rugby international (asked to play for his country at age 16 and 17) who scored 100 in 63 minutes for Lancashire v. Somerset at Bath shortly before the First World War?

219 Which two Somerset captains have captained England?

220 Which Somerset player took part in the famous "Fowler's match" between Eton and Harrow in 1910?

221 Which South African batsman did Somerset try to sign in 1965?

222 For which club (not first-class) did Chris Greetham play after being released by Somerset in 1965?

223 What was unusual about the Somerset v. Notts. Gillette Cup match at Taunton in May 1965?

224 As the result of these postponements, the original adjudicator was unable to make the presentations, only being available for the first two days. Who was he?

225 When Yorkshire dismissed Somerset for 63 in the following round of the competition what was Fred Trueman's analysis?

226 Who was the Somerset wicket-keeper who in the Gents. v. Players match at Lord's stood up to the two fastest bowlers in England, N. A. Knox and Walter Brearley?

227 Somerset awarded one county cap in 1965. Who was the recipient?

228 Who were the two Yorkshire bowlers who recorded "the ton" when Somerset scored 630 runs against them at Leeds in 1901?

229 Name the three Somerset players, a batsman, a pace bowler and a wicket-keeper who retired in 1965?

230 What milestone did Brian Langford reach in the match against Northants. at Weston-super-Mare in 1965?
231 At the same festival who took his first hat-trick in first-class cricket after 17 years in the game?
232 On Somerset's northern tour that year (1965) who scored 118 and took seven for 56 against Lancashire, following it with seven for 59 against Derbyshire?
233 When did Ken Palmer make his debut for Somerset and in what year was he capped?

234 What Somerset pace bowler was in his youth an avid attender of "the Proms" in the Albert Hall?
235 Where was he born?
236 How many wickets did he take in his two seasons with Worcestershire?
237 And how many in his first season with Somerset?
238 What was his memorable performance when opening the bowling against New Zealand at Lord's in 1965?
239 What happened to Peter Robinson's batting in 1967?
240 Who top-scored for Somerset in their first-ever Gillette Cup Final against Kent in 1967?
241 At which sport did M. M. Walford represent Great Britain in the Olympic Games of 1948?
242 When W. T. Greswell was in the Repton side of 1908 which famous cricket historian was his captain?
243 Which Somerset player while touring India in 1926-27 took part in a sixth-wicket stand of 140 in 90 minutes against Hindus at Bombay?
244 Who was his partner?
245 Who led the tour?
246 For which club did slow left armer John McMahon play for in the Central Lancashire League?
247 Who was the Somerset bowler who went to West Hartlepool in the North Yorkshire and South Durham League?
248 For which other county was J. G. Lomax capped?

28

249 Somerset had another Lomax playing for them at the same time. Who was he and what was his background?

250 In which year was Bill Alley voted Cricketer of the Year by his fellow professionals?

251 Who was the South African bowler that Somerset tried to sign in 1962?

252 For which Minor County was he playing at the time?

253 Which side was Bill Alley to be found coaching in April 1962?

TWENTY QUESTIONS — 4

254 What was Somerset's initial reaction to the Gillette Cup?

255 What took place at Taunton for the first time on December 8, 1961?

256 For which Birmingham League side did Fred Rumsey play?

257 Who was the Oxford University pace bowler registered by Somerset in 1962?

258 Which Lancashire League club attempted to sign Bill Alley to succeed Garfield Sobers as their professional in 1962?

259 Who was Harold Stephenson's 1000th first-class victim in first-class cricket?

260 When did Harold Stephenson retire?

261 Bertie Buse's benefit match against Lancashire in 1953 was over in a day. Can you name another cricketer whose benefit against Somerset lasted a similarly brief period?

262 In 1963 a Somerset player's benefit realised a record sum. Who was he and who was the previous record beneficiary?

263 On May 27, 1964, Somerset at 215 for nine defeated Nottinghamshire 215 all out in a Gillette Cup match. Who was Man of the Match?

264 Which Somerset wicket-keeper was born at Billingham?

265 Which Football League side did he play with?

266 What representative honours came the way of Harold Stephenson?

267 For which club did he play league cricket before coming to Somerset? (He played in Durham).

268 What is the highest score ever made in first-class cricket on the Glastonbury ground?

269 An opening batsman of the late 60s and early 70s, he came from Killinghall in Yorkshire. Who was he?

270 How old was Ian Botham when he achieved the Test double and how many matches did it take him?

271 Which Somerset amateur of the 20s and 30s was known as "Box"?

272 Which cricketer born at Wellington played for Somerset although it turned out to be Wellington, New Zealand?

273 Who was known as "The Colonel"?

274 Who was the early Somerset professional who had a melodrama produced on the London stage?

275 With what county had the writer played as an amateur?

276 Why was he allowed to leave Gloucestershire?

277 In which game at Taunton did the opposition's last man come to the wicket in a blue pin-striped suit?

278 Who used to turn up for matches in the 1920s dressed in top hat and morning coat?

279 How did he spend his Sundays?

280 At which match (post-World War Two) did the Somerset pros hire a donkey and cart, borrow sombreros and pretend to be visiting South Americans?

281 Who was denied a collection at a home game after scoring 310 runs because "that's what he's paid to do"?

282 Which two Kent players conspired to give Wally Luckes his only first-class century?

283 Which county captain, enquiring of his partner if he should appeal against the light at Weston-super-Mare, received from him the reply "I can hear you m'lord, but I can't see you."?

284 In which match was an angel (almost) caught fiddling?

285 Whose remedy for cramp in the legs was to rub them with whisky?

286 When Jack Hobbs broke W. G. Grace's record of centuries at Taunton in August 1925 was he compiling his 83rd, 127th or 141st?

287 How many centuries had he previously made that season?

288 What Somerset batsman scored a century in that same match?

289 Who succeeded Jack White as captain of Somerset?

290 Which Somerset cricketer was a one-time bouncer in a Sydney dance hall?

291 What do H. Gimblett, K. Palmer, Arthur Wellard, Maurice Tremlett, Harold Stephenson and L. C. H. Palairet all have in common?

292 In 1946 Somerset recorded three successive scores of 500 or over. Who were the opponents in these three matches?

293 Who did Somerset defeat in the 1967 Gillette Cup semi-final?

TWENTY QUESTIONS — 6

294 Which Somerset player is being described here by John Arlott? "With his precise manner, high forehead, dignified step and trim moustache he looked completely unlike the Bath Rugby full-back and natural games player that he was".

295 Who once took a wicket for Somerset in a first-class match wearing evening-dress shoes?

296 Did C. R. M. Atkinson ever score 1000 runs in a season for Somerset?

297 Who was the second-eleven bowler called up to play against Sussex in the Gillette tie of 1964 at Taunton who became Man of the Match?

298 Only two of the Somerset Gillette Cup final side of 1967 had played in every match for the county since the competition started in 1963. Who were they?

299 Viv Richards with 4745 runs is the John Player League highest aggregate scorer for Somerset. Who comes second?

300 What other players have scored more than 3000 runs in the John Player League, now Refuge Assurance League?

31

301 How many times have Somerset reached the semi-finals of the one-day knock-out competition, i.e. Gillette and Nat. West?

302 At the beginning of season 1988 what is their overall record in matches won and lost in this competition since 1963?

303 A Somerset cricketer, still playing first-class cricket has scored over 1000 runs for the county in this competition. Who is it?

304 Of the current staff who has the highest average in this competition (qualification — having played five matches or more)?

305 At the end of 1986 only one bowler on the staff had taken half as many wickets as Ian Botham in the Gillette and Nat. West competitions. Who was it?

306 Who holds the Somerset record for carrying his bat through a completed innings?

307 Which Somerset captain made a century on his debut for the county?

308 Who made five first-class centuries before lunch in 1901?

309 On how many occasions did Viv Richards score a century before lunch?

310 Name the two players who made centuries against touring teams on their debut for the county?

311 How many times did Ian Botham hit 10 or more sixes in an innings for Somerset in a county match?

312 Who has recorded the fastest-ever hundred for Somerset?

313 Who has scored the fastest double century?

314 Name the three players who have twice scored 2000 runs in a season entirely for Somerset.

315 Four players have scored 1000 runs ten times or more. Name them.

316 What have Brian Close, Bill Alley, Viv Richards, Colin McCool and Greg Chappell in common?

317 Two other players have done this. Who were they?

318 Harold Gimblett leads the Somerset centurions with 49 100s' then comes Viv Richards with 47. Who comes next?

319 How many first-class centuries did M. M. Walford make for Somerset?

320 And Sunil Gavaskar?

321 Who is the oldest man to have made a century for Somerset?

322 Who is the oldest man to have done the double?

323 Who is the oldest man to have made his debut for Somerset?

324 He had previously played one first-class match for another county. When was this and what was the county?

325 Which amateur (of 1910 vintage) had the longest name of any Somerset player?

326 Only three players have ever achieved the double twice in Somerset matches only. Who are they?

327 Who is the Yorkshire player who against Somerset recorded the only instance of a player scoring a century in each innings and taking five wickets in each innings?

328 Who is the player who in four separate matches against Somerset scored a century and took ten wickets?

329 Six times in Somerset matches a bowler has taken all ten wickets in an innings, twice for and four against. Name the bowlers.

330 What is the best bowling analysis against Somerset by a member of a touring side?

331 How many wickets did Brian Langford take in the three matches of the Bath Festival of 1953 which marked his first-class debut?

332 How many Somerset bowlers have been called for throwing?

333 Only one player has made more than 500 first-class appearances for Somerset. Who is he?

TWENTY QUESTIONS — 8

334 Who comes second to Brian Langford in first-class matches played for the county?

335 What is the lowest total that Somerset have recorded against another county?

336 And the lowest total for which they have dismissed another county?

337 At the end of 1986 only two counties had always recorded three-figure totals against Somerset in county matches. Who were they?

338 Who has the best Somerset bowling analysis in the Sunday League?

339 From which county did reserve wicket-keeper R. J. Blitz come?

340 How many first-class victims had he with Somerset?

341 How much did Ian Botham's benefit realise?

342 In which country and for what side has Neil Burns played overseas cricket?

343 What was Ian Botham's soccer club as a player in the Football League?

344 Who is the West Ham United supporter on the Somerset staff?

345 Who follows Tottenham Hotspur?

346 And Hull Rugby League Club?

347 Of which town is Ian Botham a freeman?

348 The holder of the amateur batting record in the Central Lancashire League scored 132 against Somerset at Old Trafford in 1985. Who was he?

349 Who was best man at Viv Richards' wedding?

350 What book did Ian Botham pick to take with him to his desert island on the programme *Desert Island Discs*?

351 For which county did one of Wisden's Five Cricketers of 1986 take nine for 56 against Somerset in 1981?

352 What unusual non-cricketing feat did Ian Botham perform on a May afternoon in 1982?

353 Which England slow bowler had recorded, at the start of the 1987 season, both his best batting and bowling performances against Somerset?

354 For which first-class overseas team has Nigel Felton played?

355 Who in his first match for Yorkshire had as his first victim in county cricket Sunny Gavaskar, then with Somerset?

356 That bowler has a famous cricketing uncle. Who is he?

357 Which eight Somerset brothers, including a capped county player, played with the same club side in Somerset?

358 Who was the former Durham University captain who scored 153 runs against Somerset in 1986 for Worcestershire?

359 Who is Dougal and why would he remember the match against Somerset at Taunton in 1977?

360 On which ground did Simon Dennis record his best bowling performance for Yorkshire — five for 35 against Somerset in 1981?

361 With which Football League reserve side did Colin Dredge play?

362 Richard Coombes best bowling performance for Somerset was recorded on his debut. Who were the opposition and what were his figures?

363 Which current Somerset player coaches at Haringay sports centre?

364 Which of the Somerset staff lists rearing pheasants as one of his recreations?

365 Name the England captain whose highest score has been recorded against Somerset at Bath.

366 On which current Somerset player did Roy Marshall have a profound coaching influence?

367 Trevor Gard's best batting performance for Somerset has been against a touring side. Can you give details?

368 Has Joel Garner ever scored a first-class century in England?

369 What size of boots does Joel Garner wear?

370 What was Trevor Gard's job outside cricket?

371 And that of Joel Garner?

372 Which current Somerset player has turned out for Durban Pirates in South Africa?

373 What is the name of the debilitating tropical disease from which he suffered for six years?

374 What is Mark Harman's nickname?

375 Where was he born?

376 Which member of the Somerset double team of 1979 was born in Buckinghamshire?

377 Who is the all-rounder who writes occasionally for the magazine *The Club Cricketer* and scored a career-best 124 against Somerset at Taunton in 1985?

378 Which Somerset player has as his superstition "always to salute a magpie"?

379 Who was the South African cricketer whose best bowling analysis is eight for 107 against Somerset at Taunton in 1981?

380 For which two South African provincial sides has Adrian Jones played?

381 Adrian Jones is almost inevitably Jonah to his team-mates but he has another title. What is it?

382 Adrian Jones has an unusual outside job for a professional cricketer, what is it?

383 Who described his father as "a dangerous village cricketer"?

384 For which New Zealand side did Neil Mallender play?

385 Which Somerset fast bowler has a relation recently playing with Glamorgan?

386 Who was the Sri Lankan batsman who scored 209* against Somerset at Hove in 1984?

387 Vic Marks has a cricket blue and another half-blue. For which sport did he get his half-blue?

388 Who is the player who recommended himself to his county and got his first century against Somerset at Weston-super-Mare in 1986?

389 What is Gary Palmer's job outside cricket?

390 Which Somerset player was for a time a grave-digger?

391 What unique distinction does Gary Palmer hold for Somerset?

392 Of which university does Viv Richards hold an honorary doctorate?

393 Who played for Somerset 2nd XI at the age of 13?

394 Which Lancashire batsman scored his highest total against Somerset at Bath in 1984?

395 What other record does he hold?

396 With which county is Paul Roebuck connected?

397 Who has the second-biggest benefit for Somerset?

398 Can you name the Somerset cricketer of the 1980's whose father played for Yorkshire and England?

399 Who was the Securicor salesman who took six for 36 for Surrey against Somerset in 1984?

400 Who was the son of Illtyd who took five for 56 against Somerset at Cardiff, also in 1984?

401 What was Brian Rose's best-ever bowling return?

402 What was unusual about Murray Turner's bowling?

403 Who is the player who has played his highest innings against the county that his father skippered?

404 Why did Somerset fail to achieve the double against Glamorgan in the County Championship of 1912?

Give the Christian names of these relatives or namesakes who played *together* in a Somerset side.

405 The Lees.

406 The Atkinsons.

407 The Palairets.

408 The Palmers.

409 The Roses.

410 What do Mike Denness, Brian Hardie and K. G. McLeod have in common in a Somerset connection?

411 For how many seasons did Somerset suspend operations during the Second World War?

412 Who was the Somerset player who scored a century *against* England at Old Trafford in the summer of 1959?

413 What was especially noteworthy about the century?

414 Name the Gloucestershire bowler who, in 1937 against Somerset at Taunton, took six for 26, including four of the last five wickets for nine runs.

415 When did Jack White play his last match for the county?

416 What was his very last bowling analysis?

417 In 1937 against Surrey at The Oval Somerset were all out for 166 in the second innings. How many of these did Arthur Wellard make?

418 Who was the Kent slow left armer who in his second-ever county match took six for 39 against Somerset at Gravesend in 1906?

419 Who was the Somerset player who played for the Gentlemen against the Players at Lords in 1938?

420 Why would Bertie Buse remember the match against Derbyshire at Derby in May 1935?

421 Who was the Aston Villa and England player (also with Arsenal) who played for Middlesex against Somerset at Bath in June 1938?

422 Why is this statement false: "In 1919 Jack White took six wickets before lunch on the third morning of the Middlesex match"?

423 Which then first class county did not meet Somerset in 1919 and why?

Can you supply the names for the nicknames of these famous players who have played against Somerset for touring teams.

424 The Boy from Bowral?

425 The Black Bradman?

426 Sticky?

427 The Governor-General?

428 Toey?

429 Slasher?

430 Davvo?

431 Sonny?

432 The Emperor Constantine?

433 Hubert?

434 Can you name four batting Sunday records that Viv Richards holds for Somerset?

435 At the start of season 1987 two Somerset players had performed the hat-trick in the John Player League. One was Viv Richards against Essex in 1982. Who was the other?

436 Somerset's highest score for and highest number of runs conceded have both been recorded against the same county. Which one?

437 Which is the county's most crushing and quickest win in the Benson and Hedges competition?

438 Two years later with the same venue and opposition, what world record was established?

439 Who hit Kerry O'Keeffe for 23 in an over in a Benson and Hedges match at Taunton in 1972?

440 Who were the Somerset players who set up an all-time record for the first-wicket partnership of a Benson and Hedges match at Canterbury in 1981?

441 What Somerset batsman, deputising for wicket-keeper Luckes had four victims, including two stumpings, in Lancashire's only defeat of 1947?

442 Who was the amateur who scored 264 against Hampshire at Weston-super-Mare that year?

443 Which well-known Surrey cricketer recorded his maiden century against Surrey at Taunton in August 1947?

444 Somerset lost in a day to Derby at Chesterfield in June 1947. When had the last one-day result been in the Championship and who were involved?

445 In the Bristol match against Gloucestershire, Somerset were tumbled out for 25. Only one player got double figures. Who was he?

446 Who was the Somerset amateur and captain who got his maiden century at Leicester in August 1947?

447 Who had a match analysis of eight for 86 on his first-ever appearance at Lord's in 1947?

448 Who was the bowler who took eight for 75 at Leeds in June 1947 against the side for which he would shortly play?

449 What was the connection between shipping and the South African attack of 1947?

450 Which Somerset player went on an England tour in 1947-48?

1948 — THE AUSTRALIANS AND OTHERS

451 Which Australian tourist scored his maiden first-class century against Somerset at Taunton in 1948?

452 Two other Australians also scored tons. Name them.

453 A fourth missed a century by one run. The unlucky chap was?

454 What Somerset bowler had a three-wicket maiden over against Essex at Chelmsford in August 1948?

455 Who was the Glamorgan amateur bowler who took 12 for 106 in the match against Somerset at Swansea in May 1948?

456 Who were the two Middlesex batsmen who put on 424 for the third wicket against Somerset at Lord's in 1948?

457 Who was the Sussex bowler who took 14 wickets at Weston-super-Mare against Somerset in August 1948?

458 What Somerset bowler took four wickets in five balls (including the hat-trick) against Yorkshire?

459 Harold Gimblett had two century partnerships while making 310 v. Sussex. His partners?

460 When Yorkshire were skittled at Harrogate for 74 in June 1948, who was their opener who scored 50% of their runs?

THE SUNNY SUMMER OF '49

461 What was significant about Maurice Tremlett's 104 against Essex at Clacton in August 1949?

462 Who was the Glamorgan bowler who destroyed Somerset with twelve for 94 at Neath in June 1949?

463 In the same month who took eight Hampshire wickets for 63 at Portsmouth?

464 A month before Northants, set to get 64, had lost eight wickets in doing so. Who skippered them for the first time that day at Taunton?

465 In another May match at Taunton why were Somerset especially pleased to beat Hampshire?

466 What was the feature of the game against Gloucestershire in June?

467 What was his match analysis?

468 In the match with Middlesex at Bath in June a player appeared who was still playing county cricket in the 1980s. Identify him.

469 His career was so long that on that day he played with the father of one of his later captains. Name father and son?

470 Who performed the hat-trick in Horace Hazell's benefit?

GROUNDS

On which Somerset grounds would you find:

471 The Ridley Stand?

472 The Rugby Stand?

473 The Stragglers Pavilion?

474 The Uphill end?

475 The Sports Centre end?

INSIGNIA

476 What is the badge of Somerset?

477 What are the club colours?

478 How would you recognise a capped second-eleven Somerset player?

479 What were the colours of the county benefit tie of 1985?

480 How many of the badges of other first-class counties depict animals as a major part of their insignia?

Give the counties for which the following players turned out before coming to Somerset.

481 P. Robertson.

482 D. J. S. Taylor.

483 D. Breakwell.

484 D. B. Close.

485 J. Parks.

486 J. Lawrence.

487 J. G. Lomax.

488 J. J. E. Hardy.

489 N. Burns.

490 N. Mallender.

HORACE HAZEL

491 How many wickets did Horace Hazel take in his benefit season 1949?

492 How many wickets did he take in Bertie Buse's benefit match against Lancashire in 1953?

ODDITIES

493 How many counties did A. A. Jones, the Somerset pace bowler of the early 1970s, assist?

494 Who was the Major who took 14 for 70 against Yorkshire at Leeds in 1895 and then scored 102 against them in 1892?

495 Who kept wicket for Somerset Stragglers on his 75th birthday?

496 Who was the regular Somerset opening batsman who was killed in Normandy during the D-Day invasion?

THE BIG-HITTING AMATEUR

497 Guy F. Earle — what was his middle name?

498 He began to play for Somerset in 1922. He had previously appeared in county cricket. When and with whom?

499 On which overseas tour did he go?

500 What was his fastest-scoring innings for Somerset?

CAPTAINS THEN AND NEARER NOW

501 What were the first names of S. S. Rogers?

502 Against which touring team did he score a century?

503 When did Brian Rose make his debut for Somerset?

504 Whom did he succeed as captain?

505 In which year was he one of Wisden's Players of the Year?

506 In which year did he begin to open regularly for Somerset?

507 What was Brian Close's best bowling performances in the John Player League?

508 What records do Somerset captains hold in the John Player League?

FOR WHOSE BENEFIT

509 Who was the Somerset cricketer who would not play on a Sunday, even in his own benefit matches?

510 His benefit match against Surrey was rain-ruined. How did the county help him?

511 What were his bowling returns in his benefit match?

512 How long did he play with Somerset and how many first-class wickets did he take with them?

F. S. LEE

513 What piece of cricket history was he part of in 1931?

514 And in 1938?

515 And how did he hit the headlines in 1960?

516 What were the details of his notable innings for Somerset v. Australia in 1934?

517 How many first-class centuries did he score?

518 What did Jeremy Lloyds and Vic Marks have in common besides off-spin bowling and a Somerset cap?

519 And what is the link between Bunty Longrigg and Colin Atkinson besides the Somerset captaincy?

520 And what did M. D. Lyon and B. H. Lyon have in common?

521 We mentioned E. F. Longrigg — what was his highest score for the county?

522 Who was the Sunderland goalkeeper who scored 201 for Somerset against Kent at Taunton in 1909?

WALLY LUCKES

523 How many victims did Wally Luckes have in the course of his wicket-keeping career with Somerset?

524 What season did he miss entirely through illness?

525 How old was he when he retired?

526 Did he make a first-class century?

M. D. LYON

527 How many times did M. D. Lyon appear for the Gentlemen against the Players?

528 Who was the famous Australian bowler whom he savaged in making 136 against the tourists at Taunton in 1926?

529 How many centuries did he hit in county cricket?

530 What did the D. in M. D. Lyon stand for?

J. C. W. MACBRYAN

531 What were his first names?

532 Why could he only field close to the wicket?

533 In his Somerset career did he make more than 5,000, 10,000, 15,000 or 20,000 runs?

534 How many centuries did he score?

COLIN McCOOL

535 In which years did he play for Somerset?

536 How many Test centuries did he make?

537 How many runs did he make and wickets did he take in England?

538 How old was he when he made his debut for Somerset?

539 What were the initials of his son who also played with Somerset and when did he turn out for them?

R. C. N. PALAIRET

540 What did his initials signify?

541 He was a double blue of Oxford University. At which other sport besides cricket did he gain this award?

542 After he finished playing, of which county did he become secretary?

543 Who was his co-manager on the 1932-33 tour of Australia?

544 What was his highest score for Somerset?

THE RIPPONS

545 Give the initials of the Rippon brothers who opened the batting for Somerset immediately before and after the First World War?

546 What did these initials stand for?

547 How many wickets did Bertie Buse take in his benefit match against Lancashire which was lost in a day at Bath in 1953?

548 What were the scores and match aggregate in the above match?

549 Name the three counties for whom Tom Cartwright appeared?

550 What were the first names of the between-the-wars amateur C. C. C. Case?

551 How many centuries did he make for Somerset and what was his highest score?

552 What was the middle name of Greg S. Chappell?

553 Who was the grandfather of the Chappells who played Test cricket for Australia?

554 In what seasons was Greg Chappell a Somerset player?

555 What were the names of his two brothers who also played for South Australia?

556 In Somerset's first season in the John Player League what home grounds did Chappell and his team-mates play on besides Bath and Taunton?

BRIAN CLOSE IN 1974

557 In 1974 Brian Close became only the sixth player in first-class cricket to make 30,000 runs and take 1000 wickets. Who were the others?

558 Why was the match against Middlesex at Taunton in July 1974 a landmark in Close's career?

559 With whom and against whom did he establish a record fourth-wicket partnership for the county?

560 He established a record in the John Player League by hitting 19 sixes in a season. Who had previously held the record?

561 Who was the coach who said of him "He plays as hard for us as he ever did for bloody Yorkshire. I can pay him no greater compliment"?

MISCELLANEOUS

562 What were the first names of the Bath and Somerset amateur batsman of the 1920s S. G. U. Considine?

563 Did he ever score 1000 runs in a season?

564 Who was the Yorkshire-born batsman from Gildersome who scored 1107 runs for Somerset in 1948?

565 Which Somerset cricketer at the age of 46 made 174* and 108 against Essex at Taunton in 1925?

566 For how many seasons did John Daniell captain the county?

567 How many rugby caps did he win for England?

568 Who was the Somerset player who captained England at Rugby and became President of the Rugby Union?

569 When Horace and Bertie were operating in tandem in the 1930s who were the Somerset bowlers?

570 Who was the Somerset bowler who played for Argentina against M.C.C. in 1912 and took 31 wickets for Somerset in 1920?

571 Who is the tallest man ever to have played Test cricket?

572 G. C. Gill who in 1902 made 804 runs and took 79 wickets for Somerset played for two other counties. Can you name them?

JOEL GARNER

573 Where was Joel Garner born?

574 Which West Indian Test bowler corrected Garner's bowling action when he was a young cricketer?

575 With what Lancashire League club did Joel Garner play?

576 How many wickets did he take during Somerset's Gillette Cup-winning run of 1979?

577 Who was the Australian Test batsman that he bowled with his fifth-ever ball for Somerset?

THE WORCESTER AFFAIR

578 In 1979 how did Somerset ensure that they would qualify for the quarter-finals when playing against Worcester?

579 What was the outcome of this decision?

580 What rule had Somerset broken?

581 Only one county voted to retain Somerset in the competition. Which county was it?

582 What were the actual scores?

583 Who scored both Worcestershire runs?

584 What makes the occasion unique in Somerset history?

585 Sunil M. Gavaskar — what does the M. stand for?

586 Which of his uncles played Test cricket for India?

587 How many first-class games had he played before being capped for his national side?

588 How many Test runs did he make in his first Test series (against West Indies in the Caribbean in 1971)?

589 What is the nickname by which he is widely known?

MORE OF HAROLD GIMBLETT

590 Gimblett made a century in his benefit match. Who were the opposition and what was the venue?

591 How did *Punch* mark his fastest century of the entire season in his very first match against Essex at Frome in 1935?

592 For what other reason was his benefit match notable?

593 According to Gimblett himself, how much money did he make from his benefit match?

594 He failed to record a century against only two counties, what were they?

595 Did he ever play abroad?

OCCASIONAL PLAYERS

596 What did the T. stand for in W. T. Greswell?

597 What was his career span with Somerset?

598 He made one first-class century. Against whom and on what ground?

599 What was Montagu L. Hambling's one performance of note for Somerset?

CLOSE SHAVES — THE GILLETTE CUP

600 Who was the bowler who took six for 15 against Somerset at Taunton in 1965 without using his full quota of overs?

601 Which Gillette match was postponed so often that Somerset's opponents played a complete county champion-ship match before it could be played off?
602 Which Somerset bowler in three separate Gillette ties bowled 36 overs for an aggregate analysis of eight for 37?
603 How many times have Somerset won matches in the Gillette Cup by virtue of having scores tied but having lost fewer wickets?
604 Who were Somerset's first opponents in a Gillette Cup final?

FESTIVALS

605 What is the highest individual score recorded on the Bath ground and who made it?
606 At which Weston Festival did Somerset fail to score three figures once in two completed matches?
607 In the match against Glamorgan at Bath in 1979 the first four Somerset batsmen all got 50s in the first innings. Who were they?

SOMERSET BORN

All the following players are Somerset born and played for the county in the last 20 years. Identify them by their town or village.

608 Glastonbury.
609 Crewkerne.
610 Chewton Mendip.
611 Frome.
612 Nailsea.
613 Paulton.
614 Kilve.
615 Middle Chinnock.
616 South Petherton.
617 Weston-super-Mare.

The following players were Somerset born but played for other counties. Name the counties.

618 M. Bissex born in Bath?

619 K. Snellgrove born at Shepton Mallett?

BOOKS AND WRITERS

The following books were written by Somerset players or supporters. Identify the authors from the titles.

620 I Don't Bruise Easily?
621 Sixty Years of Somerset Cricket?
622 It Sort of Clicks?
623 First Among Equals?
624 Harold Gimblett — Tormented Genius of Cricket?

BILL ALLEY

625 How old was Bill Alley when he joined Somerset?
626 In what year did he turn out for Players against Gentlemen?
627 For which Australian State side did he play in Sheffield Shield cricket?
628 And for which league cricket sides in England?
629 When was he capped for Somerset, and how many matches had he played?
630 How many runs did he make against the touring Australians of 1961?
631 In which match did Alley open the bowling and batting and also keep wicket?
632 In which year was he voted the players' Cricketer of the Year?
633 Which trophy did he win in that year?
634 How many runs did he score and how many wickets did he take in the course of that season?

MISCELLANEOUS

635 Amateur status was officially abolished in 1962. Who were the last Somerset players to be officially so designated?
636 Name the player who kept wicket for Bath Cricket Club for

more than 50 years and appeared for the county between 1908 and 1923?

637 Which Somerset player wrote the book *The Hand that Bowled Bradman?*

638 For how long did Colin Atkinson skipper Somerset?

639 Who was the Somerset amateur, son-in-law of John Daniell, who played for Winchester and Oriel and was reported missing, presumed killed in Malaya, in 1942?

640 Who was G. F. D. Battle and why did he make Wisden in 1971?

641 Who was the amateur who in the 1930s acted as R. A. Ingle's vice-captain and scored 735 runs in 1934?

642 How did Bertram Lewis Bisgood mark his debut for Somerset in first-class cricket?

BOTHAM

643 How many wickets did Ian Botham take in his first day of Test cricket?

644 How old was he on his Test debut?

645 What was remarkable about his innings against Hampshire in the Benson and Hedges quarter-final of June 1974?

646 What bowling feat marked his first two test matches?

647 When did he make his debut for Somerset?

LEN BRAUND

648 Which counties did Len Braund play with before joining Somerset?

649 How often did he perform the double for Somerset?

650 How many times did he go to Australia?

651 Which side did he coach after he stopped playing?

652 What type of bowler was he?

653 What did he do on his retirement from playing?

654 What misfortune befell him in 1943?

655 What honour came his way in 1949?

656 In what famous partnership was he involved against Yorkshire in 1901?

657 How many Test centuries did he score in Australia?

MISCELLANEOUS

658 With whom did J. J. Bridges toss up for the number eleven batting spot in the Somerset side of the 1920s?
659 Two players made centuries in Graham Burgess's Testimonial match in the John Player League against Derbyshire in 1972. Who were they?

MIXED BAG

660 What occasional Somerset batsman of the 1970s was a noted discus and shot putt exponent?
661 Who was the Australian slow-left-arm bowler, previously with Surrey who came to Somerset in the 1950s?
662 And the surname of the slow-left-arm bowler who had previously played for Yorkshire and whose first name was Ellis?
663 Who was the famous West Indian cricketer who recommended Hallam Moseley to Somerset?
664 How old was Brian Close when he was recalled to the England side against West Indies in 1976?
665 Who was the umpire who warned Michael Holding for delivering three consecutive bouncers at Close in a Test?
666 On which New Zealand ground did Ian Botham score a century, take eight wickets and hold three catches in a Test match?
667 What did Graham Yallop pioneer at Bridgetown, Barbados, against West Indies in 1978?
668 What is the name of Sunil Gavaskar's brother-in-law who was also a Test cricketer?
669 What record did Greg Chappell set at Perth against England in 1974-75?

670 This is a photograph of the Somerset side of 1895. Can you name the captain (seated in centre of middle row)?

671 This is a photograph of two famous Somerset skippers in very much later life. Can you identify them?

672 Who are these two most famous of early Somerset batsmen?

673 Bowler and batsman, both Somerset. Who are they?

674 Schoolmaster and county captain. Who be he?

675 The greatest Somerset hitter of all time, Botham excepted. Identify him.

676 He got rid of Bradman . . . eventually. Who was the persevering bowler?

677 He straddled the Second World War . . . and the wicket.
678 A Somerset fast bowler with an inappropriate name.

679 Who is the portly footballer being congratulated in this photograph?

680 In this same photograph who is the goalkeeper?

681 Can you name the three players in this football side who captained Somerset?

682 Why did this cricketer make history at Taunton in August 1925?

683 The favourite recreation of this spin bowler was stag-
hunting. Whose is the picture?

684 An unforgettable style. Not too difficult to name this young
Somerset batsman.

685 Can you identify the Middlesex fielders?

686 Which two counties are involved in this match?
687 And who are the two players concerned?

688 How many England players are there in this group of Somerset taken in 1975?

689 Who is the little-known Somerset player on the extreme right of the middle row?
690 And the player third from the right of the middle row?

691 This player was a hard-hitting batsman and one of Somerset's very first imports. Who was he?

692 And another highly successful import but much more recent.

693 This is the Australian whose signing saw the county leave
the foot of the championship after four years. Name him.

694 Portrait of the artist as a young man. Almost too easy.

695 The Bicknoller Boy but what was his Sunday name?

696 Nagging bowler, adhesive bat and county coach. What is he
called?

697 Somerset were famous for the large number of amateurs
they fielded between the wars. There are five on the front
bench alone of this 1922 side. Can you name them?

698 And this front row of 1930?

699 Harold Gimblett driving characteristically against Middle-sex. Who are the admiring fielders?

700 Demolition job! Who is the enthusiastic wicket-keeper?

701 Gentlemen and players: Can you identify the six professionals in this side which played Kent at Dover in 1937?

702 And their five unpaid colleagues?

703 He captained and was President of the county. What is his
name?

704 Possibly the best Somerset opening batsman post-war, though Peter Roebuck and Graham Atkinson fans might argue differently. Who is he?

705 Journalist, county cricketer and committee man. What's his name?

706 Who is the bowler deep in thought at the end of the over?
707 And the wicket-keeper bustling away?

708 This stylish left-hander is now on the umpires list?

709 Who is the Somerset player on the extreme right of the back row in this team group of 1967?

710 What is the name of the secretary in the front row?

711 Two players, fifth and fourth from the right in the back row have almost the same name. Who are they?

712 Can you identify the players second, third and fourth from the left in the back row?

713 Who is this determined young bowler?

714 Not how most Somerset followers would remember him.
Who is he?

715 This pace bowler won two Man of the Match awards in his first eight Gillette Cup appearances. Who is he?

716 Pad up lads! A captain who pre-eminently led by example.

717 He came from the obscurity of second-eleven cricket to become Man of the Match against Sussex in the Gillette tie of 1964. What is his name?

718 Not a lot of doubt about this one. Who's on his way back?

719 Roy Virgin is the batsman here but who is the fielder crouching in front of the square-leg umpire?

720 Who is the tall left-armer bringing out a forward defensive shot from this Hampshire batsman?

721 Who is the receiving Hampshire batsman?

722 And the non-striker?

723 Down memory lane. Who is the leader (extreme right) of this peculiarly rustic group?

724 Who forgot to duck?

725 Danger, world-class batsman at work. Identification please?

726 Why did Peter Denning receive the Concorde award in 1980?

727 Who is this man deep in thought and where is he?

728 On the great walk. Ian Botham and Mike Gatting are instantly recognisable but who is the third party?

729 Sesquipedalian difference. Or, if you prefer, a foot and a half. Who are the long and short of it?

730 "Honestly, you haven't changed a bit!" Reunion of three Somerset stalwarts of the 1930s. Who are they?

731 Who is this contemporary member of staff?

732 Familiar faces but where is the strange place?

733 Great crowd rapport. Who is the Somerset player who has made the members forget that six?

734 Often more important than any player and a Somerset stalwart.

735 Who is the sad loser on the balcony?

736 This is the life! Who is the player in the lap of luxury?

737 Two well-known Somerset fans celebrate victory. Their names?

738 Great promise unfulfilled. A batsman in the classic vein.

739 Not just a bunch of amateurs, there's a World Cup player here. Who?

740 Which side did Vic Marks captain at an early stage of his career?

741 One Somerset great beats another. Under what circum-
stances?

742 Peter Denning played the key innings in the semi-final of
the Gillette Cup of 1979. How many, and who were the
opposition?

743 Is the batsman out twice? Well, the wicket has gone and he's apparently caught behind. By whom?

744 Portrait of a very useful bits and pieces man. Who?

745 What part did Colin Dredge play in the two great days of
the 1979 season?

746 Just made it! Who got back and when?

747 Lightning bat seen as demon bowler. Who is this great trier?

748 This young bowler bears a famous Somerset name. Who is he?

749 This Somerset player was one of four caps awarded during 1987. Who is he?

750 Why the extravagant rejoicing by Ian Botham?
751 Who is the batsman just dismissed?
752 Who is the umpire giving the decision?

753 The man in the centre of the front row is Somerset's first captain in first-class cricket. Who is he?

754 There are eight amateurs in this Somerset side of 1926. Name them.

755 And the three lonely professionals.

756 Identify these two stalwart Somerset openers.

757 And these ones.

758 He toils not but he spins. Who is the left-armer?

759 The strong side of 1946 with the skipper in civvies. Name him.

760 A slight look of Bill Edrich about this leg-side shot but who is the Somerset batsman?

761 Maurice Tremlett bowling against
Australia in 1948. Who is batting?

762 Who is the non-striker?

763 Tremlett batting with an unusually tall wicket-keeper.
Name the stumper.

764 Top edge for which Yorkshire batsman?
765 Who is standing at first slip for Somerset?

766 Good-bye Smithson! Who are the admiring fielders?

767 Stephenson stumps Ken Graveney, much to the admiration of . . .?

768 The West Indies against Somerset 1950. The small man on the far left of the back row would become world famous in the course of the summer. Who was he?

769 How many first-class umpires from this Somerset team group of 1961?

770 The beneficiary of 1962 had a Lancashire connection.

771 Barry Meyer of Gloucester is the victim. Who is the bowler?

772 What did both men subsequently have in common?

773 And what does Ken Palmer have in common with this fellow?

774 Who is about to deliver?

775 An early view of the county ground. What is the name of
the church in the foreground?

776 Name the back row of this staff photograph of 1964.

777 Photograph of a cricketer, wit and writer. Who is he?

778 These three players parted with Somerset in 1966. Who are
they?

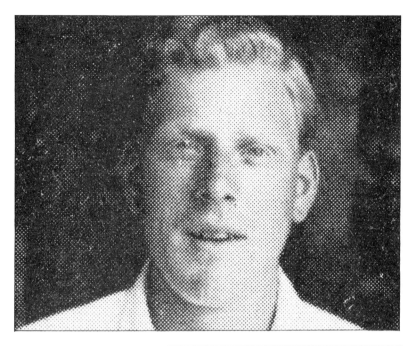

Can you identify the following ties. Most of them, but not all, are benefit ties.

779

780

781

782

783

784

785

786

103

787   788

1950 — THE YEAR OF THE CALYPSO

789 Who were the two West Indians who got centuries in the tour match at Taunton in May 1950?

790 Which Glamorgan player scored a century in each innings at Cardiff?

791 In this match which other Glamorgan player recorded his first century?

792 Harold Gimblett was picked against West Indies. Why didn't he play?

793 Who was the noted Kent opener who made his last ever appearance against Somerset at Gravesend in June 1950?

794 Name the England captain who scored 120* in the Yorkshire second innings at Taunton in August of that year.

795 A Somerset second-line bowler took five for 50 in the first innings against Surrey at The Oval in August. Who was he?

796 Who got a double hundred for Sussex at Worthing against Somerset in July 1950?

797 Who was the little-known Somerset opening bowler who took four for 66 and two for 39 against Warwickshire at Edgbaston in July 1950?

798 Where was the away match played against Yorkshire in 1950?

1951 — FESTIVAL OF BRITAIN—AND OTHER FESTIVALS

799 What happened in the last hour of the South Africa match at Taunton?

800 In the Gloucestershire match at Bristol in August, a home batsman scored a century in each innings. Who was he?

801 Middlesex batsmen scored heavily against Somerset at this time. Who was the opener who in 1951 scored 232* at Lord's?

802 In 1951 Maurice Tremlett hit the highest score of his county career. What was it and who were the opposition?

803 Who was the Gloucestershire Test batsman who made his maiden century against Somerset at Taunton in May 1951?

804 In this season Somerset lost to a county they dismissed for 52 in the first innings. Name the county and the venue.

805 What two records did Jack Robertson of Middlesex set at Taunton in July 1951?

806 Which future Somerset bowler had his career-best analysis, 15 for 78 in the match against Somerset at the Weston Festival?

807 When Somerset beat Surrey by 67 runs at The Oval it was their first win against them in London since when?

808 Who scored more than 2000 runs in county cricket for Somerset?

1952

809 Who scored his maiden century against the Indian touring team?

810 Who did likewise at Swansea against Glamorgan?

811 Which Somerset bowler took six for 16 as Middlesex slumped to 52 all out at Bath?

812 During the Bath Festival Harold Stephenson had a rare off-day against Warwickshire. How many byes did he concede?

813 Against which county did Gimblett score a century in each innings?

814 Who was the Somerset coach who had to umpire for part of Harold Gimblett's benefit match?

815 Doug Insole figured in an unusual dismissal in the second innings of the match at Taunton in July. How was he out?

816 Which Somerset amateur scored his maiden century against Hampshire at Taunton in August?

817 Who scored a double century for Surrey at The Oval?

818 In June, John Langridge scored a century against Somerset at Hove, his 69th. In doing so he set up a Sussex record. Who had previously held it?

CORONATION YEAR—BUT NOT FOR SOMERSET!

819 A Test captain and a famous fast bowler scored centuries for the Australians at Taunton in August 1953. Identify them.

820 Two counties defeated Somerset twice in the season by an innings. Which counties were they?

821 One of Somerset's few successes was a 10-wicket win at Lord's. Who was the little-known bowler who took four for 38 in their first innings?

822 Who was the Australian bowler who took 12 for 48 for Notts against Somerset in August 1953?

823 How many defeats did Somerset suffer in the 1953 season?

824 Who hit three consecutive centuries against Northamptonshire in the seasons 1952 and 1953?

825 What bowler had an analysis of 26 wickets for 97 runs in the two matches against Somerset?

826 Who were the Warwickshire pair who put on 275 for the fourth wicket at Coventry in May 1953?

827 Four Somerset players scored 1000 runs in county cricket.

Gimblett, Stephenson and Tremlett were three. Who was the other?

828 Who kept wicket for the Australians at Taunton?

1954—HAIL AND FAREWELL

829 Who was the Pakistan batsman who, listed at number eleven and not batting in the first innings, scored 135 at Taunton in the second?

830 Who was the opener who scored a century first time round?

831 A Somerset opener got a century in the same match. Who?

832 An Essex bowler with a famous name took five for nine at Southend in August. Who was he?

833 In how many championship matches did Harold Gimblett play before retiring?

834 What were his scores in his very last county appearance?

835 Who captured his wicket on both occasions?

836 Who was the Somerset beneficiary of 1954 who missed the double by 98 runs and nine wickets?

837 When Somerset defeated Nottinghamshire at Taunton in May 1954 when was the last time they had won at county headquarters?

838 What was remarkable about the 1954 Bath Festival?

THE YEAR 1955

839 Who was the South African captain who, batting at number eight, rescued his side with 87* at Taunton?

840 Who was the Somerset batsman who hit his maiden century against Essex at Romford while suffering from acute appendicitis?

841 Who was the Notts wicket-keeper who made four stumpings, two off Goonesena, two off Smales, at Trent Bridge in July 1955?

842 In what area of batsmanship did Somerset, bottom in 1955, excel the county champions Surrey?

843 Name the Somerset five.

844 For which county did B. E. Disbury and J. Spanswick play against Somerset?

845 Who took 15 for 95 in a match against Somerset and finished on the losing side?

846 How many victims did Harold Stephenson have against Worcestershire in July 1955?

847 Who were the two Yorkshire left-handers who put on 191 for the second wicket at Taunton in July 1955, each scoring a century?

848 Who had his first hat-trick in the match against Somerset during the Weston Festival of 1955?

1956—AN AUSTRALIAN YEAR

849 Who was the Australian who scored a century in each innings against Somerset at Taunton in July 1956?

850 Who had been the last Australian to score a century in each innings in a match in England?

851 In the Somerset match name the two other Australian batsmen who also scored a century.

852 Why was 1956 a landmark in the social history of the club?

853 Who took five for eight in a new-ball spell against Derbyshire at Derby?

854 Who in 1956, in his second match for Somerset, scored his maiden county century against Glamorgan at Cardiff?

855 What unwanted distinction did Somerset acquire in August against Hampshire?

856 Name the reserve Somerset wicket-keeper who in his first match scored 56* out of 148 all out at Old Trafford.

857 Which two Australians put on 123 at Trent Bridge for the Notts last wicket?

858 Who had a match analysis of 10 for 120 against Essex at Taunton in May?

1957—THE WAY BACK

859 Somerset dismissed West Indies at Taunton for 78 in the

tour match. Name the two bowlers who divided the wickets.

860 Who took six for 29 in the innings victory over Derbyshire in August at Chesterfield (second innings)?

861 Only three Somerset-born players turned out for the county in 1957. One was Roy Virgin. Who were the other two?

862 In which match did Bill Alley take 10 for 61?

863 Whose match analysis was nine for 31 when Lancashire rolled over Somerset in two days at Old Trafford?

864 Name the two Somerset bowlers who split the wickets in dismissing Leicestershire for 41 in July 1957.

865 Which Somerset bowler took 81 wickets in the season at an average of 21.44 and was not re-engaged?

866 What distinction did Bryan Lobb achieve in 1957?

867 In the Bath match against Hampshire who was the visiting player who was given out run out, recalled and his partner adjudged out and later, in another incident, run out himself?

868 Who was the Australian bowler who took seven for 60 in his debut match against Glamorgan at Weston in 1957?

THE MIDDLE 'FIFTIES

869 In the last month of his county career Johnny Lawrence had the highest score of his first-class career. Against whom and how many?

870 In his last match against Sussex at Hove he was given a reception by the crowd who were also saying farewell to two noted Sussex players. Who were they?

871 How many wickets did Brian Langford take in the three games of the Bath Festival in 1956?

872 Who was the bowler who performed the hat-trick during the Festival?

873 Who were the two young Yorkshire bowlers who shared all 10 wickets against Somerset at Taunton in July 1956?

874 Who were the two bowlers of the same name who took 22 of

the 34 wickets to fall in the Lancashire match at Weston in August 1956?

875 Name the Northamptonshire batsman who in the 1950s scored three successive centuries against Somerset?

876 Who, in two innings scored 190 out of Somerset's match aggregate of 355 against Surrey at The Oval without being dismissed?

877 Who took five for eight in the second innings against Cambridge University at Cambridge in May 1957?

878 And the Somerset bowler who took seven for 63 in the University's first innings?

THE YEAR 1958

879 Who scored 161 for New Zealand against Somerset at Taunton in May 1958?

880 In the win against Essex at Ilford who scored 130* in the second innings and who took eight for 67 in the Essex second innings?

881 Who made 130 against Glamorgan at Cardiff in May?

882 Against which county did Somerset lose five wickets at the same total?

883 Who had the best bowling analysis of his career against Notts at Trent Bridge?

884 Who after the Taunton match against Surrey had scored 533 runs against them in three consecutive innings?

885 Who made his first century in first-class cricket against Somerset at Sheffield?

886 And which Somerset player scored his maiden century against Warwickshire at Taunton?

887 Who performed the hat-trick for Somerset at the Weston Festival?

888 Who took 12 for 52 against Glamorgan, also at Weston?

MORE FROM THE 'FIFTIES ... AND 'SIXTIES

889 In 1958 against Worcester at Taunton, Colin McCool fell to the second ball bowled in county cricket by . . .?

890 Who took 15 for 54 against Lancashire at Weston in 1958 and what were the Lancashire totals?

891 What Somerset player was capped in 1958?

892 What did Denis Silk, Bill Alley and Geoff Lomax have in common in the first innings of the match against Surrey at The Oval?

893 Who was the player, later with Somerset, whose 101* won the match for Warwickshire at Edgbaston in May 1959?

894 Name the two Leicestershire batsmen who established a record third-wicket stand for their county in the match at Taunton against Somerset in 1961?

895 Name the two future England captains who played in the Cambridge side against Somerset in 1961?

896 Who made 104 in 100 minutes for Warwickshire at Street?

897 How many sixes did he hit?

898 Name the three Lancashire players who scored centuries in the second innings of the match at Weston-super-Mare?

1959—THE YEAR OF UNBROKEN SUNSHINE

899 Which of the Indian tourists scored a double century at Taunton in May 1959?

900 Who scored his first century in first-class cricket for Somerset at Derby?

901 Who was the Middlesex opener, "something in the City", who got a century in the Lord's match of June 1959?

902 When Arthur Milton scored 103 against Somerset at Taunton in May, what landmark had he reached on the county ground?

903 Against Middlesex at Bath, Peter Wight helped to set a county record partnership of 196 for the sixth wicket. Who was his partner?

904 The high spot of the season for Somerset was an innings of 222*. Who played it and against what opposition?

905 In the match against the Combined Services who scored his initial century in first-class cricket?

906 Who hit 128 in the Yorkshire first innings in a losing cause at Bath?

907 Name the England opening pair who put on 191 for the first Surrey wicket against Somerset at The Oval in May 1959.

908 Which two players scored centuries in the same innings in a match which Somerset lost?

909 Who was the South African slow-left-arm bowler who took 12 for 119 in the match at Taunton in June 1960?

910 What was significant about Somerset's win at Cardiff in 1960?

911 Who was the Somerset bowler who was no-balled five times for throwing in the match against Gloucestershire at Bristol?

912 Who was the umpire who called him?

913 Who were the two Middlesex openers of the same name who each scored a century against Somerset at Glastonbury in July?

914 Who established what county record in the game against Glamorgan at Bath?

915 Who had held the previous record?

916 What record did Peter Wight set against Warwickshire at Weston in August?

917 Name the three amateurs who assisted Somerset in 1960.

918 Peter Wight scored 2316 runs in all first-class matches thereby establishing a new county record. Who had previously held it?

919 Who was the future Somerset captain who had a match-winning performance of five for 23 in the second innings of the Gentlemen v. Players match at Lord's?

920 In which match did a Somerset innings last less than sixteen overs?

921 Which match did Somerset lose after establishing a first-innings lead of 201?

922 Who was the bowler who took 11 for 72 against Gloucester-shire at Bristol?

923 Who scored a double century for Hampshire at Bournemouth?

924 Who was the Leicestershire slow bowler who performed the hat-trick?

925 Who was the Middlesex captain who made the first 50 of his career against Somerset at Lord's?

926 Who hit his maiden century for Somerset at Northampton?

927 Who took five wickets for one run in 31 balls for Hampshire at Frome?

928 What Somerset batting record was set against Surrey at Taunton by Bill Alley?

THE YEAR 1962

929 Which touring side did Somerset defeat by an innings and 86 runs?

930 Against which county did Peter Wight take four for 11?

931 In which match did Somerset score a match aggregate of 168 and win by nine wickets?

932 Who was the Somerset bowler who took 10 for 48 in the match?

933 Who was the Test umpire who carried his bat for Leicestershire although only making 26*?

934 Who was the England captain who, while playing for Cambridge University, scored two centuries against Somerset?

935 Where was the away match against Leicestershire played in 1962?

936 Who was the bowler who took a career-best seven for 54 with leg-breaks against Gloucestershire at Taunton?

937 Who was the Middlesex spinner who destroyed Somerset with 12 for 86 at Weston?

938 Who was the Somerset wicket-keeper who opened the batting with Mervyn Kitchen against Cambridge University at Fenners?

939 Who in 1961 scored a double century for Somerset in a county match which was lost?

940 Also in 1961 Ron Headley made 150* against Somerset at Dudley. Why might this innings have given him particular pleasure?

941 Who was the massive Kent bowler, later an umpire, who drove a bubble-car and was hurt in a crash before the match at Weston in 1962?

942 Who was the Warwickshire bowler, later with Somerset, who took 10 for 72 against them at Weston in 1962?

943 How many matches were there in the Weston festival of 1962?

944 Who were the two Worcester batsmen who set a third wicket county record of 314 against Somerset at Worcester in 1962?

945 Who was the Yorkshire player who in 1963, skippering his county for the first time, took seven catches and made 46 against Somerset at Harrogate?

946 Who was the BBC sports commentator who was run out on 99 while playing for Glamorgan at Weston in 1965?

947 In that same season, 1965, what Somerset player scored two centuries in a losing game?

948 Who in 1965 carried his bat for Somerset at Hull?

949 Who were the two West Indians who scored centuries for the tourists in the match at Bath in May 1963?

950 What was unusual about the away match with Derbyshire in 1963?

951 Who took twelve for 59 in the match against Glamorgan at Neath?

952 Somerset won by an innings in a county match of 1963 despite scoring only 156. Who were their opponents?

953 Who was the Hampshire leg-spinner who took ten wickets in the match at Bournemouth?

954 Who won the match for Somerset at Old Trafford by taking 11 for 73 and scoring 45 runs in an innings?

955 Who conceded 23 runs off his first two overs against Nottinghamshire at Trent Bridge and finished with figures of nine for 57?

956 Who was the Worcestershire slow-left-arm bowler who at Bath in June 1963 took six for 12?

957 In 1963 who scored two not-out centuries in the Glastonbury match?

958 Which Somerset slow left armer took 11 for 102 against Derbyshire during the Weston Festival?

1964—AN AUSTRALIAN YEAR

959 Which Australian scored a century for the tourists at Taunton in May?

960 Which Somerset secretary took eight for 76 in the match with Gloucestershire at Bristol in August 1964?

961 Who was the opener who carried his bat in the second Hampshire innings at Bournemouth?

962 Who took ten for 78 on a "duster" at Bath against Gloucestershire?

963 Name the West Indian who took four for 8 in seven overs for Lancashire in Somerset's second innings at Bath?

964 Which Somerset player carried his bat in the first innings against Glamorgan at Weston-super-Mare?

965 Who was the Derbyshire player who scored a century at Taunton in August?

966 Who was the future Somerset county coach who took seven for 28 against Somerset at Coventry in the first innings in May 1964?

967 When Fred Rumsey was picked for England against Australia at Old Trafford he was the third Somerset player to be selected since World War Two. Who were the others?

968 What prominent Somerset player retired in 1964?

969 New Zealand and South Africa (for the last time) visited. Which Kiwi scored a century at Taunton in June?

970 Who took the last four Essex wickets at Westcliff without conceding a run?

971 Which Somerset player scored a century in both Middlesex matches?

972 Who followed an 83* with five for 46 against Middlesex at Lord's?

973 Which Northamptonshire bowler took 12 for 56 at Northampton in the match in June 1965?

974 Which Somerset bowler took six for 60 against Nottinghamshire at Worksop?

975 Who, coming in as a night watchman, scored his maiden century against Gloucestershire at Bristol?

976 Who was the New Zealander who played with some success for Somerset after the 'Varsity match?

977 Who scored 73* in 45 minutes against Cambridge University at Taunton in June?

978 Who bowled unchanged in the Hampshire match at Bath?

1966—THE OTHER WORLD CUP YEAR

979 Two West Indians got centuries against Somerset at Taunton in July, one a double century. Who were the successful batsmen?

980 Who made his debut for Somerset in 1966? As a clue, he was an all-rounder whose bowling became the stronger of his attributes.

981 In the match against Derbyshire at Burton-on-Trent, Harold Rhodes, the Derbyshire bowler, was called for throwing. By whom?

982 His action was passed from the other end. Who was standing there?

983 Why was May 15, 1966, a special day in the annals of Somerset?

984 August 16 was also a special day that season. Why?

985 Who scored the last half century on the ground?
986 Graham Burgess took part in a century partnership in his first county championship match. Where and against whom?
987 Can you give Roy Palmer's and Bill Alley's bowling analyses in the Gillette Cup semi-final against Warwickshire?
988 What unprecedented bowling feat did Somerset achieve in 1966?

MOSTLY 1966 AGAIN—A BUSY YEAR

989 In 1965 (note date) who took 8-26 against Hampshire at Bath?

All following questions refer to 1966.

990 Who made his maiden hundred in the away match with Worcestershire?
991 What record did Roy Virgin establish?
992 Whose figures were 20.1–9–26–8 against Gloucestershire at Bath?
993 Which Somerset bowler took 24 wickets in the Bath Festival of 1966?
994 Which player, later prominent with Essex, took four for 44 for Cambridge University at Taunton in June 1966?
995 At which sport did he represent Great Britain in the Olympic Games?
996 When Brian Langford had Mushtaq Mohammed of Northants caught by Bill Alley at Glastonbury what landmark had the bowler reached?
997 Who performed the hat-trick at the Weston Festival of 1966?
998 In 1966 Somerset established a record number of championship victories. How many matches did they win?
999 Who had the top score of 71 in the Sussex second innings against Somerset at Eastbourne in August?

Answers

CAPTAINS COURAGEOUS

1 Samuel Moses Joseph Woods, 1894-1906.
2 John Daniell 1908-12, 1919-26.
3 R. J. O. Meyer and C. R. M. Atkinson.
4 Ben Brocklehurst.
5 J. C. White 1927-31.
6 D. R. W. Silk.
7 G. G. Tordoff.
8 G. E. S. Woodhouse, J. W. Seamer, N. S. Mitchell-Innes.
9 E. F. Longrigg 1938-46.
10 Brian Close for Yorkshire in 1949.

COUNTY GROUNDS

11 Frome, against Essex.
12 Wells. Derbyshire were champions in 1936.
13 Westland and Johnson's.
14 The Imperial Ground. Also Knowle and Brislington.
15 Six for 25 against Glamorgan in 1972.
16 The Recreation Ground.
17 Torquay.
18 It was decided that there should be no county ground!
19 The Avon and the Tone, respectively.
20 To J. C. White.

THE COUNTY CHAMPIONSHIP

21 They were played over two days only.
22 For that season only there was an experiment with eight-ball overs.
23 Against Sussex at Taunton in 1919, Heygarth was the Sussex batsman involved.
24 Derbyshire at Chesterfield.
25 Lancashire at Bath (Bertie Buse's benefit match).
26 Bill Alley in 1962.
27 One, Jim Parks who kept for England when with Sussex.
28 Nine.

29 Jeremy Lloyds.

30 322 by Viv Richards against Warwickshire at Taunton in 1985.

JOHN PLAYER LEAGUE

31 At Trent Bridge, Nottingham.

32 At Yeovil.

33 A. A. Jones.

34 Brian Langford whose analysis against Essex at Yeovil in 1969 was 8–8–0–0.

35 Nigel Popplewell at Bath v. Glamorgan in 1983 and Viv Richards against Sussex at Horsham in 1986.

36 Hugh Gore.

37 34 wickets in a season in 1974.

38 Middlesbrough, against Yorkshire.

39 Four for 21 at Bath in 1981.

40 175* (13 sixes) against Northamptonshire at Wellingborough in a match which was abandoned in August 1986.

FANCY CAPS

41 Walford, Langdale, Watts.

42 Baig, Case, Powell.

43 J. H. Cameron who played in the Test series in England in 1939.

44 J. C. MacBryan, M. D. Lyon, J. C. White and R. C. Robertson-Glasgow.

45 F. H. McRae.

46 S. S. Rogers.

47 H. T. Gamlin whose analysis was two for 182 in that match in 1895.

48 H. T. Hewett.

49 Richard Palairet.

50 P. R. Johnson with two against Middlesex in the same match, 164, 131, and 117 against Hampshire and 126 against Kent.

51 R. C. Robertson-Glasgow.

52 Peter Denning.

53 Graham Burgess.

54 Colin Dredge.

55 Joel Garner.

56 J. C. White.

57 S. M. J. Woods.

58 M. D. Lyon.

59 Brian Roe.

60 Phil Slocombe.

BILL ALLEY

61 Eleven.

62 Sixty-two.

63 He had 28 fights and won them all.

64 He scored 183 not out followed by 134 not out. No Somerset player had ever compiled two not-out centuries in the same match.

65 134 followed by 95 not out.

66 Ten. The other was made for A. E. R. Gilligan's XI v. the Australians.

67 Only two: Jack Hobbs and Frank Woolley.

68 None. He recorded a pair against Glamorgan at Weston-super-Mare.

69 Graham Atkinson.

70 93.

MORE NICKNAMES

71 N. S. Mitchell-Innes.

72 Maurice Tremlett.

73 Geoff Clayton.

74 Peter Roebuck.

75 Dennis Breakwell.

A VARSITY MATCH

76 All four innings produced century opening partnerships, a feat unparalleled in first-class cricket.
77 R. M. Prideaux, later of Kent, Northants and Sussex.
78 Peter Wight who scored 105 in the first innings and 99 in the second.
79 Graham Atkinson 103 and Roy Virgin 113.
80 A. R. "Tony" Lewis — later of Glamorgan.

JOHN CORNISH WHITE

81 47 years, from 1891 to 1937.
82 Against Worcestershire in matches at Worcester and Bath.
83 Twice, in 1929 and 1930.
84 He took 391 catches altogether.

OVERSEAS ALLEGIANCES

85 Griqualand West.
86 Western Australia.
87 Central District and Auckland.
88 The Leeward Islands.

R. C. ROBERTSON-GLASGOW

89 Raymond Charles.
90 Charterhouse.
91 Four.
92 From 1919 to 1937.
93 Nine for 39 against Middlesex at Lord's in 1924.
94 The famous amateur cricketer C. P. McGahey of Essex.
95 G. Young with whom he put on 160 against Essex at Knowle and 139 against Worcester at Taunton, both in 1928.

WHOSE BENEFIT?

96 A. E. Trott of Middlesex.

97 In the second innings he took four wickets in four balls and later on in the innings he performed the hat-trick — this at Lord's in 1907.
98 Driving a ball over the present pavilion at Lord's.

ARTHUR WELLARD

99 From 1927 to 1950.
100 Frank Woolley of Kent.
101 "Much better be a policeman".
102 To India.
103 Stan McCabe.

JACK WHITE

104 In November 1928 in the Test match there he bowled six overs of which two were maidens and took four wickets for seven runs.
105 A. P. F. Chapman.
106 It was a timeless test and lasted for eight days, at that time the longest duration ever for a cricket match.
107 13 wickets for 256 runs.
108 2361 wickets at 18.58 and 12,152 runs at 17.89.

NICKNAMES AND TERMS OF ABUSE

109 Paul Bail (from his initials P. A. C).
110 Mark Davis.
111 Jeremy Lloyds.
112 Neil Mallender.
113 Gary Palmer.
114 Not Brian but Graham Rose.
115 That's Brian Rose.
116 Murray Turner.
117 Julian Wyatt (for obvious reasons).
118 Nigel Felton.

FOR AND AGAINST

119 Jonathan Atkinson.

120 Paul Bail.

121 Phil Bainbridge, with eight for 53.

122 R. J. Bartlett with 117* against Oxford University in 1986.

123 Richard Blakely.

THE UMPIRES LIST OF 1987

124 J. H. Harris and Alan Whitehead.

125 John Jameson of Warwickshie.

126 A. A. Jones (possible uncomplimentary reference to his fielding!).

127 A. A. Jones who played with Sussex, Somerset, Middlesex and Glamorgan.

128 Mervyn Kitchen, formerly with Somerset.

129 Ken and Roy Palmer.

130 Both played for Somerset.

131 Neither of them. Ken was born at Winchester and his younger brother Roy at Devizes.

132 In South Africa in the tour of 1965.

133 Peter Wight (Somerset).

134 In 1966.

135 He had three brothers of whom G. L. Wight played for West Indies while H. A. Wight and N. Wight both played for British Guiana.

THE YEAR 1966

136 Some of them had an experimental first-innings limitation of 65 overs.

137 At Ilford against Essex on May 15.

138 Peter Robinson.

139 It was the last county championship match to be played at Cardiff Arms Park.

140 He took 42 catches, constituting a county record.

HARD-LUCK STORIES

141 W. T. Greswell who in a span of twenty years appeared regularly in only three seasons.

142 J. C. W. MacBryan — against South Africa in 1924 at Old Trafford.

143 J. C. W. MacBryan.

144 The Invicta of Kent.

PETER WIGHT

145 222 against Kent at Taunton in 1959.

146 Harold Gimblett with 2134 runs in 1952.

147 Only one season. He was overtaken by Bill Alley in 1961.

148 Georgetown, British Guiana.

149 Both men appeared on the first-class umpires list.

THE 'SEVENTIES

150 Philip Slocombe.

151 Roy Virgin.

152 David Gurr.

153 Viv Richards and Peter Roebuck.

154 Tom Cartwright of all people!

COUNTY CHAMPIONSHIPS

155 Lancashire.

156 Counties had the option by agreement of playing "late hours", that is from 1.30 p.m. to 8.15 p.m.

157 20.

158 32.

159 In 1979 when they lost for the first time in the last game of the season against Sussex at Hove.

TESTERS

160 Martin Crowe and T. C. Lowry in the 1920s.

161 Sunil Gavaskar and Abbas Ali Baig.
162 Colin McCool, Greg Chappell, Steve Waugh, Kerry O'Keeffe.
163 H. W. Stephenson.
164 Yes. A one-day international against Sri Lanka at Taunton in 1983.

ENEMY DEEDS

165 Buckinghamshire.
166 Mike Gatting who scored 258 in 1984 and 196 in 1987.
167 Bill Edrich and Denis Compton.
168 Richard Hadlee for Nottinghamshire against Somerset at Trent Bridge, August 1987.
169 424 by A. C. McLaren of Lancashire in 1895.

HAROLD GIMBLETT

170 Dorset.
171 The Lawrence Trophy awarded for the fastest century of the season.
172 The Old Trafford Test of 1950 against West Indies. He was never selected for England again.
173 He was attached to the National Fire Service.
174 Millfield.

HOME AND AWAY

175 Both captains, Ian Botham and Viv Richards together with both umpires, Bill Alley and Ken Palmer, had Somerset connections.
176 Greg Chappell in the fifth Test of 1973 at the Oval.
177 Sunil Gavaskar.
178 The Bradford League.
179 C. W. Grove.
180 Middlesex.
181 Wicket-keeper Leslie Compton bowled and kept wicket alternately for the first eight overs of the second innings.

182 A. Fairbairn with 108 in the second innings.

183 L. B. Fishlock.

184 Eric Bedser who scored 154.

MISCELLANEOUS

185 In the course of it he had a partnership of 144 with A. E. S. Rippon thought to be the only time that twins have shared in a century partnership in first-class cricket.

186 Six.

187 J. C. P. Madden-Gaskell.

188 A. E. Newton.

189 Jack Redman.

190 Frank Ashley Phillips.

191 Sir S. Ponsonby-Fane.

192 At Beckenham.

193 Tom Richardson.

TWENTY QUESTIONS — I

194 Graham Stevenson who hit him for seven sixes, Crowe's final analysis being 6–0–70–0.

195 H. N. E. "Granny" Alston at The Oval in 1933.

196 Bobby Abel.

197 811.

198 At Hastings, playing for a Commonwealth XI against an England XI.

199 Richard Ollis.

200 Hockey.

201 Rugby Union football.

202 For greyhound racing.

203 N. S. Mitchell-Innes at Killermont, Glasgow, in 1931.

204 Stuart Turner of Essex with 121 at Taunton in 1970.

205 Peter Willey (now of Leicestershire) at Northampton in 1976.

206 With Roy Virgin, formerly of Somerset, Willey put on 370 for the fourth wicket to establish a new county record.

207 145 against Oxford University in 1985.

208 Millfield.
209 Sherborne.
210 Millfield (as coach).
211 Downside.
212 Millfield (as head).
213 Christ's Hospital as pupil, Marlborough as teacher, Radley as headmaster.

TWENTY QUESTIONS — 2

214 He was a member of the M.C.C. tour to Canada.
215 Nigel Popplewell (Mr. Justice Popplewell).
216 John Daniell, in asking Robertson-Glasgow to bowl four more deliberate wides into a geranium bed at Bath against Yorkshire in the 1920s. Owing to a quirk in the points allocation, Yorkshire were deliberately trying to avoid taking first-innings lead in a rain-shortened match.
217 D. J. Mordaunt who made 60 of Berkshire's 137, Somerset winning with 139 for five.
218 K. G. McLeod.
219 J. C. White and I. T. Botham.
220 G. F. Earle. The match is so-called because Fowler top-scored in the Eton second innings then with Harrow needing 55 to win he took eight for 23, Eton winning by nine runs.
221 Graeme Pollock.
222 He was pro. with Torquay.
223 It was the first match in the competition to use all three allotted days.
224 F. R. Brown of England, Surrey and Northants.
225 Six for 15.
226 H. Martyn.
227 Wicket-keeper Geoff Clayton.
228 George Hirst whose figures were 37–1–189–1 and Wilfred Rhodes 46.5–12–145–6.
229 Batsman Peter Wight, pace bowler Geoff Hall and wicket-keeper Peter Eele.
230 He took his 1000th wicket in first-class cricket.

231 Fred Titmus.
232 Ken Palmer.
233 He first played in 1955 and was capped in 1958.

TWENTY QUESTIONS — 3

234 Fred Rumsey.
235 Stepney in London.
236 Eleven.
237 102.
238 He took the first four wickets for seven runs in 46 balls.
239 Promoted from number nine in the order to number one he responded by scoring 917 runs.
240 Peter Robinson with 48 runs.
241 Hockey.
242 Harry Altham.
243 G. F. Earle.
244 Maurice Tate of Sussex.
245 A. E. R. Gilligan, also of Sussex.
246 Castleton Moor.
247 Ken Biddulph.
248 Lancashire.
249 I. R. Lomax of Eton Ramblers and Wiltshire.
250 In 1962.
251 Cuan McCarthy.
252 He was currently with Dorset.
253 Cambridge University.

TWENTY QUESTIONS — 4

254 They voted against participation in it.
255 Greyhound racing.
256 Kidderminster.
257 J. D. Martin.
258 Radcliffe.
259 Bomber Wells, caught off Rumsey v. Nottinghamshire, May 8, 1963.
260 1964.

261 Flower of Middlesex whose benefit match began and ended on May 23, 1899.
262 Peter Wight whose benefit raised £5000. Previously Harold Stephenson with £4040.
263 Maurice Hill of Notts. with an innings of 107.
264 Harold Stephenson.
265 He was on the books of Darlington during the Second World War.
266 He was a member of the M.C.C. A Team Tour to Pakistan 1955-56.
267 Stockton C.C.
268 187* by Alan Jones of Glamorgan who in the same match made 105 in his other innings.
269 Tony Clarkson.
270 23 years of age, 21 Test matches.
271 C. C. C. Case.
272 T. C. Lowry, the New Zealand Test player.
273 Somerset's first captain in first-class cricket, H. T. Hewlett.

TWENTY QUESTIONS — 5

274 G. B. Nichols.
275 Gloucestershire.
276 He once dropped four catches in a day and was told by W. G. Grace "You shall never play for us again!"
277 Against Sussex at Taunton in 1919 the last man, Heygate had changed because, suffering from arthritis, it was thought unlikely that he could bat. He took so long to get to the wicket that on appeal he was given out and the match ended as a tie.
278 P. Johnson.
279 In bed, reading Dickens.
280 Against Essex at Clacton 1949. The South Americans won by an innings and fifty runs!
281 Harold Gimblett after making 310 v. Sussex at Eastbourne in 1948. The county secretary of the time turned down the request.
282 Leslie Ames and Frank Woolley. Ames found out in the 90s

that Luckes had never scored a first-class century and induced Woolley to bowl.

283 Lord Tennyson of Hampshire.

284 Les Angell was caught behind by Ken Fiddling, the Northants wicket-keeper in the match at Frome in 1950.

285 S. M. J. Woods.

286 127th.

287 13.

288 J. C. W. MacBryan.

289 R. A. Ingle.

290 Bill Alley.

291 They never played for any other first-class county.

292 India, Middlesex and Yorkshire.

293 Lancashire at Old Trafford.

TWENTY QUESTIONS — 6

294 Bertie Buse.

295 R. C. Robertson-Glasgow.

296 Yes, in 1966 he scored 1120 runs at an average of 26.04.

297 Geoff Hall who took five for 34.

298 Bill Alley and Roy Virgin.

299 Peter Denning with 4565 runs.

300 Ian Botham, Brian Rose and Peter Roebuck.

301 Eight times.

302 Played 60, won 37, lost 23.

303 Viv Richards.

304 Nigel Felton.

305 Colin Dredge with 60 wickets to Botham's 88.

306 It is shared by L. C. H. Palairet and Len Braund, both of whom accomplished this feat on four occasions.

307 D. B. Close with 104* against Leicestershire at Leicester in 1971. He was then 40 years of age.

308 L. C. H. Palairet.

309 On two occasions, 117* not out against Lancashire at Southport in 1977 and 102 against Glamorgan at Taunton in 1986 when his century occupied a mere 58 minutes.

310 M. M. Walford with 141* v. India in 1946 and P. B. Wight with 109* v. Australia in 1953.

311 Four times: hitting 10 v. Gloucester at Taunton in 1980; v. Warwickshire at Taunton in 1982; v. Northants at Weston-super-Mare in 1985; and 12 v. Warwickshire at Edgbaston in 1985.

312 N. F. M. Popplewell in 41 minutes against Gloucestershire at Bath in 1983. He went on to score 141 in 62 minutes.

313 S. M. J. Woods in 135 minutes against Sussex at Hove in 1895. He was out having scored 215 in 150 minutes.

TWENTY QUESTIONS — 7

314 Harold Gimblett, Graham Atkinson and Peter Wight.

315 Harold Gimblett, Peter Wight, Bill Alley and Viv Richards.

316 All scored 1000 runs in their first season with Somerset.

317 Phil Slocombe, and Martin Crowe.

318 L. C. H. Palairet with 27.

319 Seven.

320 Two.

321 Ernest Robson who made 111 in 1921 when he was 51.

322 Bill Alley with 1915 runs and 112 wickets in 1962 when he was 43 years old.

323 William Cecil Caesar who was 46 on his first appearance in 1946.

324 As far back as 1922 he had played in one game for Surrey.

325 Humphrey Seymour Ramsey Critchley-Salmonson.

326 Oddly all were team-mates: Jack White, Arthur Wellard and Bill Andrews.

327 George Hirst who at Bath in 1906 scored 111 and 117* and took six for 70 and five for 45.

328 J. R. Mason of Kent.

329 Jack White and Ernest Tyler of Somerset, A. Drake (Yorkshire), A. E. Trott (Middlesex), T. Rushby (Surrey) and C. W. L. Parker (Gloucestershire).

330 Nine for 38 by Bill O'Reilly of Australia at Taunton in 1930.

331 26. He took one against Lancashire, 14 against Kent and 11 against Leicestershire.

332 Two, E. J. Tyler in 1900 and L. E. Bryant in 1960.
333 Brian Langford.

334 Harold Stephenson.
335 25 against Gloucestershire at Bristol in 1947.
336 22. Also against Gloucestershire in 1920.
337 Oddly enough Northamptonshire and Warwickshire.
338 Viv Richards with six for 24 against Lancashire at Old Trafford in 1983.
339 From Essex 2nd XI in 1985.
340 Eight, all caught.
341 £90,822.
342 Western Province B in South Africa.
343 Scunthorpe United.
344 Neil Burns.
345 Graham Rose.
346 Neil Mallender.
347 Yeovil, where he went to school.
348 M. R. Chadwick.
349 Ian Botham.
350 *The Immortal Victor Trumper* by Jack Fingleton.
351 John Childs (now with Essex) for Gloucestershire at Bristol.
352 He wrote off two sports cars in successive 100 m.p.h. crashes.
353 Nick Cook of Northants who, while with Leicestershire, scored 75 against Somerset at Taunton in 1980 and two years later on the same ground took seven for 63.

354 Western Australia.
355 S. J. Dennis.
356 Sir Leonard Hutton.
357 The brothers Dredge with Frome Cricket Club.
358 Tim Curtis of Worcestershire at Worcester.

359 He is Nigel Cowley of Hampshire and he recorded his best score of 109*.
360 At Sheffield.
361 Bristol City Reserves.
362 Five for 58 against Middlesex at Weston-super-Mare in 1985.
363 Darren Foster.
364 Trevor Gard.
365 Mike Gatting with 258 in 1984. In 1987 he missed another double century on the same ground by just four runs.
366 Richard Harden. Marshall is the former West Indian and Hampshire batsman.
367 51* against India at Taunton in 1979.
368 Yes, he scored 104 against Gloucestershire at Bristol in 1980 when playing for West Indies.
369 He takes custom-built 16s which dwarf even those of Peter Roebuck whom legend credits with a modest 13.
370 He was a turner with an aircraft engineering factory.
371 He worked as a telegraph operator in the West Indies.
372 Jonathan Hardy.
373 Bilharzia (hookworm).

TWENTY QUESTIONS — 10

374 He has two, Basil or Harmony.
375 Aylesbury in Buckinghamshire.
376 Derek Taylor.
377 K. D. James of Hampshire.
378 Adrian Jones.
379 Garth Le Roux.
380 For Border in 1981-82 and for Orange Free State in 1986.
381 Quincy.
382 He is a financial consultant.
383 Vic Marks.
384 Otago.
385 Hallam Moseley.
386 Gehan Mendis, now with Lancashire.

387 From Oxford University for Rugby fives.
388 Andy Moles of Warwickshire with 102*.
389 He is a squash coach.
390 Peter Denning.
391 He is their youngest professional ever, having been given a contract at the age of 14.
392 The University of Exeter.
393 Peter Roebuck.

TWENTY QUESTIONS — II

394 Steve O'Shaughnessy with 184*.
395 On September 11, 1983, against joke bowling from Leicestershire, he equalled the fastest hundred (35 minutes) established by Percy Fender against Northamptonshire in 1920.
396 Gloucestershire.
397 Brian Rose with £71,863.
398 Nick Taylor (father Ken).
399 Dave Thomas.
400 The other Thomas, Greg.
401 Three for nine against Gloucestershire at Taunton in 1975.
402 He bowled right-arm fast medium and left-arm spin.
403 Tim Tremlett (father Maurice) who made 102* against Somerset at Taunton in 1985.
404 Glamorgan did not join the County Championship until 1921.
405 Frank and Jack.
406 Colin and Graham.
407 Lionel and Richard.
408 Ken and Roy.
409 Brian and Graham.
410 They are Scots who have scored first-class centuries in matches against Somerset.
411 Six. The years from 1940-45, inclusive, were totally lost to first-class cricket.
412 Abbas Ali Baig who scored 112 in the Indian second innings during the Manchester Test.
413 It was Baig's debut against England.

414 Walter Hammond.

415 Against Glamorgan at Weston-super-Mare in August 1937.

416 A very good one, 32–16–52–6 in a match-winning performance.

417 91*.

418 Frank Woolley.

419 R. J. O. Meyer.

420 In the second innings he scored 104, his first championship century.

421 Joe Hulme.

422 County matches were of two days duration in 1919.

423 Worcestershire did not field a side in the county championship during that season.

424 Don Bradman.

425 George Headley.

426 D. J. McGlew of South Africa.

427 C. G. Macartney of Australia.

428 Hugh Tayfield of South Africa.

429 Ken Mackay of Australia.

430 Alan Davidson of Australia.

431 Sonny Ramadhin of the West Indies.

432 Leary Constantine of the West Indies.

433 Clive Lloyd of the West Indies.

ONE-DAY STUFF

434 Most runs in a season (578), highest career aggregate (4745), most sixes in a career (146), most runs off one over (34).

435 Roy Palmer against Gloucester at Bristol in 1970.

436 Hampshire who conceded 286 for seven at Taunton in 1981 and scored 288 for five at Weston in 1975.

437 Ten wickets v. Combined Universities at Taunton in 1978. The entire match was over in 45.1 overs.

438 D. J. S. Taylor took eight catches, a feat unparalleled in a limited-overs match.

439 Mike Procter of Gloucestershire.
440 Brian Rose 137* and Sunil Gavaskar 90.

441 Frank Lee.
442 M. M. Walford.
443 Alec Bedser who hit 126.
444 Somerset again — they lost in a day to Lancashire in 1925.
445 Frank Lee who "amassed" 17 runs.
446 G. E. S. Woodhouse with 109.
447 Maurice Tremlett.
448 Ellis Robinson.
449 The Plimsoll line. J. B. Plimsoll took eight for 111 in the match at Bath.
450 Maurice Tremlett to the West Indies.

451 Ian Johnson with 113*.
452 Lindsay Hassett, 103 and Neil Harvey 126.
453 Ron Hamence.
454 Horace Hazell. '
455 S. Trick.
456 Bill Edrich with 168* and Denis Compton 252*.
457 James Langridge whose 14 for 129 included four wickets in five balls in the second innings.
458 Johnny Lawrence.
459 He put on 180 with M. M. Walford and 210 with Miles Coope.
460 H. Halliday.

461 It was his first hundred in England.
462 Len Muncer.
463 Johnny Lawrence.
464 F. R. Brown.

465 It was the first time the professional qualified for the new bonus of £5 a win.
466 Horace Hazell bowled 105 consecutive balls without a run scored.
467 Twelve for 63.
468 Freddie Titmus.
469 Horace and Mike Brearley.
470 Jack Ikin of Lancashire.

GROUNDS

471 Taunton.
472 Bath.
473 Taunton.
474 Weston-super-Mare.
475 Bath.

INSIGNIA

476 A wyvern, a mythical heraldic beast.
477 Black, maroon and silver.
478 He would have the Roman numerals XXII on cap or sweater.
479 Red, white and blue.
480 Three, the Kent Invicta (a white horse) the Warwickshire bear and the Leicestershire fox. A deer figures less prominently in the Nottinghamshire coat of arms.

PREVIOUS ADDRESSES

481 Worcestershire.
482 Surrey.
483 Northants.
484 Yorkshire.
485 Sussex.
486 Yorkshire.
487 Lancashire.

488 Hampshire.
489 Essex.
490 Northants.

HORACE HAZEL

491 He took 104 wickets.
492 Five.

ODDITIES

493 Four: Sussex, Somerset, Middlesex and Glamorgan.
494 Major, later Colonel, Sir Walter Coote Hedley, K.B.E., C.B., C.M.G.
495 A. E. Newton. He stumped five victims!
496 Jack Lee, brother of Frank Lee.

THE BIG-HITTING AMATEUR

497 Fife.
498 With Surrey for whom he played twice in 1911.
499 To New Zealand with M.C.C. in 1929-30.
500 59 in 15 minutes against Gloucestershire at Taunton in 1929.

CAPTAINS THEN AND NEARER NOW

501 Stuart Scott.
502 He scored 107* against South Africa at Taunton in 1951.
503 In 1969.
504 Brian Close.
505 1980.
506 In 1975.
507 Four for nine against Glamorgan in Mervyn Kitchen's Testimonial match in 1973.
508 Brian Langford has the most economical bowling analysis, 8–8–0–0 and Ian Botham the highest number of sixes (13) in an innings.

FOR WHOSE BENEFIT

509 Johnny Lawrence.

510 They met all the match expenses which traditionally had to be paid by the beneficiary.

511 Five for 54 and four for 81.

512 He began in 1946, finished in 1955 and took 798 wickets in total.

F. S. LEE

513 With his brothers Jack (Somerset) and Stanley (Middlesex) he got 1000 runs in a season, the first time that three professional brothers had ever done this in first-class cricket.

514 He became the first Somerset batsman to score 2000 in a season.

515 As a test umpire he no-balled Griffin of South Africa in the Lord's Test of that year.

516 He carried his bat for 59 out of a total of 116.

517 23.

COMMON INTERESTS

518 Both attended Blundell's School.

519 Both also played hockey for the county.

520 Captaincy of a first-class county, M. D. skippering Somerset and his brother B. H. Gloucestershire.

521 205 against Leicester at Taunton in 1930.

522 A. E. Lewis.

WALLY LUCKES

523 827 of which 586 were caught and 241 stumped.

524 That of 1931.

525 48.

526 Yes, batting at number five against Kent in 1937 at Bath.

M. D. LYON

527 Six times.

528 Clarrie Grimmett.

529 14.

530 Full name was Malcolm Douglas Lyon.

J. C. W. MACBRYAN

531 John Crawford William.

532 His right arm had been severely damaged in fighting at Le Cateau during the First World War.

533 10,322 at an average of 29.50.

534 18 centuries.

COLIN McCOOL

535 From 1956 to 1960 inclusive.

536 One, 104* against England at Melbourne in the 1946-47 series.

537 He made 8225 runs at an average of 33.70 and took 232 wickets at an average of 28.17.

538 He was 40 years old.

539 R. J. in 1982.

R. C. N. PALAIRET

540 Richard Cameron North.

541 Association Football.

542 Surrey.

543 Sir Pelham Warner.

544 156 against Sussex at Taunton in 1896.

THE RIPPONS

545 A. D. E. and A. E. S.

546 Albert Dudley Eric and Arthur Ernest Sydney.

547 Six wickets for 41 runs.

548 Somerset 55 and 79, Lancashire 158, a match aggregate of 292 runs.
549 Warwickshire, Somerset and Glamorgan.
550 Cecil Charles Coles Case.
551 Seven centuries with a best score of 155 against Surrey at The Oval in 1931.

GREG CHAPPELL

552 Stephen.
553 Vic Richardson.
554 1968 and 1969.
555 Ian and Trevor.
556 Weston-super-Mare (Devonshire Road), Bristol (Brislington), Yeovil, Glastonbury, Torquay.

BRIAN CLOSE IN 1974

557 George Hirst, Wilfred Rhodes, Frank Woolley, W. G. Grace and J. W. Hearne.
558 It was the first time that he recorded a pair in 26 seasons of first-class cricket.
559 With Derek Taylor in putting on 226 against Glamorgan at Swansea.
560 Stuart Leary of Kent with 17.
561 Bill Andrews.

MISCELLANEOUS

562 Sidney George Ulick.
563 No, he came close with 973 runs in 1922.
564 Miles Coope.
565 John Daniell.
566 Eleven.
567 Seven.

568 John Daniell.
569 Hazell and Buse.
570 Philip Arnold Foy.
571 Joel Garner.
572 Leicestershire and London County.

JOEL GARNER

573 Christchurch, Barbados.
574 Charlie Griffith, unlikely as it seems!
575 Littleborough.
576 17 wickets for 92 runs including six for 29 in the final.
577 Rick McCosker at Bath in 1977.

THE WORCESTER AFFAIR

578 They declared after one over so that Worcester would have
     no chance to win the section by virtue of a faster wicket-
     taking rate.
579 Somerset were disqualified for an "indefensible declaration".
580 They had not broken any competition rule but they had
     deliberately lost the match against the spirit of the game.
581 Derbyshire.
582 Somerset one for no wicket (a no ball) Worcestershire two
     for none.
583 Glenn Turner.
584 It is the only time in their history that Somerset have ever
     deliberately lost a match.

GAVASKAR

585 Manohar.
586 M. K. Mantri, who kept wicket for India.
587 Only six.
588 774 in only four tests as he missed the first one at Kingston.
589 Sunny (sometimes known as "The Little Master").

590 Northamptonshire at Glastonbury in 1953.

591 By the following piece of verse:

> *How comes it that this agricultural youth*
> *Can meet the wiliest ball and feetly scotch it?*
> *Simple and elementary is the truth,*
> *His Gimblett eye enables him to Watchet.*

592 It was the first county match ever played at Glastonbury.

593 £8.

594 Warwickshire and Yorkshire.

595 Yes, he visited India with the Commonwealth XI in the winter of 1950-51 when he made 1269 runs at an average of 39.65.

596 William Territt.

597 From 1908 until 1933.

598 Against Middlesex at Lords in 1909.

599 Against Worcestershire at Worcester in 1920 he made 58 runs (sharing a century partnership with John Daniell) and took six for 31 in the home side's second innings.

600 Fred Trueman of Yorkshire who only bowled 10.2 overs.

601 The semi-final match against Middlesex at Lord's in 1977 which was postponed for no fewer than nine days before being completed on a 15 overs per side basis.

602 Bill Alley v. Sussex 1966, v. Warwickshire 1966 v. Northants 1967.

603 Two, v. Nottinghamshire at Taunton in 1964 and Essex at Taunton in 1978.

604 Kent in 1967.

FESTIVALS

605 303 not out by Warwick Armstrong for Australia in 1905.

606 In 1955 with scores of 36 and 91 against Surrey and 37 and 98 against Hampshire.

607 Brian Rose 56, Phil Slocombe 92, Peter Denning 88 and Peter Roebuck 52 not out.

SOMERSET BORN

608 Graham Burgess.

609 L. M. L. Barnwell.

610 Peter Denning.

611 Colin Dredge.

612 Mervyn Kitchen.

613 Julian Wyatt.

614 Mark Davis.

615 Vic Marks.

616 Trevor Gard.

617 Phil Slocombe.

618 Gloucestershire.

619 Lancashire.

BOOKS AND WRITERS

620 Brian Close.

621 Ron Roberts.

622 Peter Roebuck (with Ian Botham).

623 Jeffrey Archer.

624 David Foot.

BILL ALLEY

625 38.

626 1961.

627 New South Wales.

628 Colne and Blackpool.

629 He was capped on May 25, 1957, having played five matches.

630 He scored 365 runs in four innings, 134 and 95 for Somerset v. the Australians and 102 and 34 for A. E. R. Gilligan's XI against them at Hastings.

631 Against Middlesex at Lord's in 1957.

632 In 1962.

633 The Brylcreem Trophy.

634 1915 runs and 112 wickets.

MISCELLANEOUS

635 C. R. M. Atkinson and Ian Lomax in 1961.

636 S. L. Amor.

637 Bill Andrews.

638 For three seasons, 1965 to 1967.

639 W. F. Baldock.

640 He retired as Somerset head groundsman after 50 years.

641 Major G. M. Bennett.

642 By scoring 82 and 116* against Worcestershire at Worcester in 1907.

BOTHAM

643 Five in 1977 against Australia at Nottingham.

644 21 years old.

645 He made 45* after having been hit in the mouth by a ball from Andy Roberts and losing four teeth.

646 He took five wickets in the first innings of each.

647 In 1973 with two John Player League matches.

LEN BRAUND

648 Surrey and London County.

649 On three consecutive occasions, 1901, 1902, 1903.

650 Three times, in 1901-02, 1903-04, 1907-08.

651 Cambridge University, especially their great side of 1925.

652 A leg-break bowler.

653 He was a first-class umpire from 1920-38.

654 He had to have one of his legs amputated and he lost the other one a few years later.

655 He was one of the first 26 retired professional cricketers to be made honorary members of M.C.C.

656 At Leeds he put on 222 with L. C. H. Palairet. Somerset made 630 in their second innings and recovered from a near-hopeless position to win the match.

657 Two, 103* at Adelaide in 1901-02 and 102 at Sydney in 1903-04.

MISCELLANEOUS

658 R. C. Robertson-Glasgow.

659 A. J. Borrington of Derbyshire, 101 and Viv Richards 104.

MIXED BAG

660 Richard Cooper.

661 John McMahon.

662 Robinson.

663 Garfield Sobers.

664 45 years old.

665 Bill Alley.

666 At Christchurch in 1978.

667 He wore a helmet to face Joel Garner.

668 G. R. Vishwanath.

669 He held seven catches, a record for a non-wicketkeeper in matches between England and Australia.

PICTURE QUIZ I

670 S. M. J. Woods.

671 S. M. J. Woods and John Daniell.

672 Len Braund and Lionel Palairet.

673 Hallam Moseley and Maurice Tremlett.

674 R. J. O. "Jack" Meyer who skippered the county side in the 1930s.
675 Arthur Wellard.
676 Bill Andrews.
677 Wally Luckes, pre-war and post-war wicket-keeper.
678 Bryan Lobb.

PICTURE QUIZ 2

679 Horace Hazell.
680 Arthur Wellard.
681 S. S. Rogers, Harold Stephenson and Maurice Tremlett.
682 He was J. B. Hobbs and in the match against Somerset, playing for Surrey, he first equalled and then surpassed W. G. Grace's record of 127 first-class centuries.
683 Jack White.
684 Greg Chappell in a match against Middlesex.
685 Peter Parfitt and wicket-keeper John Murray.
686 Somerset and Kent.
687 Brian Close batting and Alan Knott behind the stumps.
688 Six in all. They are Vic Marks and Jim Parks (first and second left, back row), Ian Botham and Brian Close (second left and second right, middle row) and Brian Rose and Tom Cartwright (front row).

PICTURE QUIZ 3

689 J. S. Hook.
690 R. J. Clapp.
691 T. C. Lowry, of Wellington, New Zealand. He played in the 1920s.
692 Bill Alley.
693 Colin McCool.
694 I. V. A. Richards.
695 Harold Gimblett.
696 Tom Cartwright.
697 (Left to right) from second in, W. T. Greswell, P. R. Johnson, J. Daniell, J. C. White and J. C. W. MacBryan.

148

698 C. C. C. Case, M. D. Lyon, J. C. White, R. A. Ingle. E. F. Longrigg.

PICTURE QUIZ 4

699 Leslie Compton behind the stumps and Bill Edrich at slip.
700 Harold Stephenson.
701 Hazell, Luckes, Lee, Gimblett, Wellard and Andrews.
702 J. H. Cameron, H. D. Burrough, R. A. Ingle, N. S. Mitchell-Innes, P. McRae.
703 E. F. "Bunty" Longrigg.
704 Roy Virgin.
705 Eric Hill.
706 Peter Robinson, later county coach.
707 Geoff Clayton, formerly with Lancashire.
708 Mervyn Kitchen.

PICTURE QUIZ 5

709 F. T. Willetts.
710 R. Robinson.
711 From left to right, L. M. L. Barnwell and T. E. Barwell.
712 They are Mervyn Kitchen, Graham Burgess and Tony Clarkson.
713 Ken Palmer.
714 Brian Langford, much more famous as a fine slow bowler.
715 Roy Palmer.
716 C. R. M. Atkinson.
717 Geoff Hall.
718 Graham Burgess.

PICTURE QUIZ 6

719 Colin Milburn of Northamptonshire.
720 Fred Rumsey.
721 Barry Reed.
722 Roy Marshall.
723 Adge Cutler seen here with the Wurzels.

724 Brian Rose in some distress against Sylvester Clarke of Surrey.
725 Sunil Gavaskar.
726 He was the only Somerset player to score 1000 runs for the county in championship matches.
727 Peter Roebuck during the Weston Festival.
728 Graham Botham, brother of Ian.

729 Trevor Gard and Joel Garner.
730 C. T. P. Barnwell, J. W. Seamer and N. S. Mitchell-Innes.
731 Julian Wyatt.
732 Viv Richards receiving the commemorative plate of his 322 v. Warwickshire from chairman Michael Hill at Port of Spain, Trinidad.
733 Colin Dredge.
734 Head groundsman Gordon Prosser.
735 Jim Griffiths of Northamptonshire after the Gillette 1979 final.
736 Graham Burgess after the 1979 Lord's final (Gillette).
737 John Cleese and the late Pete McCombe.
738 Phil Slocombe.

739 Viv Richards who has represented his country at World Cup level in soccer.
740 Oxford University.
741 Viv Richards defeats Greg Chappell in the final of the Blackthorn Trophy in September 1979.
742 He made 90* v. Middlesex at Lord's.
743 D. J. Taylor.
744 Keith Jennings.
745 He missed the Gillette final through injury but was part of the team which took the J. P. L. trophy at Trent Bridge next day.

746 Viv Richards early in his innings against Northants in the Gillette final of 1979.

747 Nigel Popplewell who retired much too soon from first-class cricket.

748 Jonathan Atkinson, son of Colin Atkinson.

749 J. J. E. Hardy, formerly of Hampshire.

750 He has just broken Denis Lillee's test bowling record.

751 Jeff Crowe of New Zealand.

752 David Sheppard.

753 H. T. Hewett.

754 Back row, numbers 3, 4, 5, from left, R. C. Robertson-Glasgow, C. C. C. Case and E. F. Longrigg. Front row, G. F. Earle, P. R. Johnson, J. Daniell, J. C. White, M. D. Lyon.

755 Frank Lee, Young and Hunt.

756 Frank and Jack Lee.

757 J. C. W. MacBryan and Young.

758 Horace Hazell.

759 E. F. Longrigg.

760 Harold Gimblett, hooking characteristically.

761 Lindsay Hassett.

762 Sid Barnes.

763 Leslie Compton of Middlesex.

764 N. W. D. Yardley.

765 Arthur Wellard.

766 Johnny Lawrence and, behind the wicket, Wally Luckes.

767 Ellis Robinson at slip.

768 Sonny Ramadhin.

769 Three, Ken Palmer, third from left, back row, and Bill Alley and Peter Wight, on right of front row.

770 Geoff Lomax.

771 Ken Palmer.

772 Both became test umpires.

773 He is Bill Andrews and they both did the double in championship matches, Andrews in 1938 and Palmer, next Somerset man to do so, in 1961.

774 Jack White.

775 St James.

776 R. Paull, R. C. Kerslake, T. I. Barwell, D. Doughty, F. T. Willetts.

777 R. C. Robertson-Glasgow.

778 From left to right: Graham Atkinson, Chris Greetham and Brian Roe.

PICTURE QUIZ 12

779 The Derek Taylor benefit tie.

780 The "Double" tie of 1979, Gillette Cup and the John Player League.

781 The Viv Richards benefit tie.

782 The Brian Rose benefit tie.

783 The Colin Dredge benefit tie.

784 The Hallam Moseley benefit tie.

785 The Peter Denning benefit tie.

786 The Joel Garner benefit tie.

787 The club centenary tie.

788 The Wyverns tie. The Wyverns are supporters of Somerset who live and work outwith the county.

1950 — THE YEAR OF THE CALYPSO

789 Frank Worrel 104 and Clyde Walcott 117*.

790 Gilbert Parkhouse with 121 and 148.

791 Len Muncer, 114.

792 He withdrew because of a carbuncle on his neck.

793 Leslie Todd.

794 N. W. D. Yardley.

795 J. Redman.

796 John Langridge 241.

797 J. Conibere.

798 At Huddersfield.

1951—FESTIVAL OF BRITAIN—AND OTHER FESTIVALS

799 In August 1951 Somerset needing 65 runs with eight wickets standing saw all eight go down for just 40 runs.

800 George Emmett.

801 S. M. Brown.

802 185 against Northamptonshire at Northampton.

803 Arthur Milton.

804 Derbyshire at Frome in June 1951.

805 He was first batsman to 2000 runs and the only one to have reached this figure every year in the seven seasons since World War Two.

806 Ellis Robinson.

807 1904.

808 Maurice Tremlett.

1952

809 Johnny Lawrence, 103* at Taunton in May 1952.

810 Harold Stephenson, 114.

811 Horace Hazell.

812 43. There were 14 byes in the first innings and 29 in the second.

813 Against Derbyshire at Taunton in July, 146 and 116.

814 H. W. Parks, formerly of Sussex.

815 Stumped Gimblett, bowled Smith.

816 G. G. Tordoff with 101*.

817 Bernard Constable with 205* in July 1952.

818 C. B. Fry with 68 centuries.

CORONATION YEAR—BUT NOT FOR SOMERSET!

819 Lindsay Hassett 148, and Alan Davidson 104*.

820 Derbyshire and Nottinghamshire.
821 C. G. Mitchell.
822 Bruce Dooland.
823 19 out of 28 in the county championship.
824 Harold Gimblett.
825 Bruce Dooland of Nottinghamshire, 10 for 49 and 12 for 48.
826 F. C. Gardner and H. E. Dollery.
827 A former amateur, R. Smith.
828 Don Tallon.

1954—HAIL AND FAREWELL

829 Shuja ud Din.
830 Hanif Mohammed, 140.
831 F. L. Angell.
832 J. A. Bailey (no relation to T. E.).
833 Two.
834 None and five against Yorkshire.
835 Freddie Trueman.
836 Johnny Lawrence.
837 In 1950.
838 For the first time since the Second World War, Somerset lost all three matches.

THE YEAR 1955

839 Jack Cheetham.
840 M. Walker with 100 in the second innings.
841 E. J. Rowe.
842 Five Somerset batsman scored 1000 runs in county matches as against only two for Surrey.
843 Tremlett, Wight, Tordoff, Lawrence and Stephenson.
844 For Kent at Yeovil in June 1955, Somerset won by three wickets.
845 Fred Titmus of Middlesex at Bath, June 1955.
846 Eight, all caught.
847 D. B. Close with 143 and J. V. Wilson with 109*.
848 Tony Lock of Surrey.

849 J. W. Burke, 138, 125*.

850 Alan Kippax against Sussex at Hove in 1930.

851 I. D. Craig, 100* and Colin McCool, 116 for Somerset. He too narrowly missed the double with 90 in his first innings.

852 For the first time there was a professional captain, M. Tremlett.

853 K. D. Biddulph who had five for 46 in the innings altogether.

854 D. R. W. Silk in the first innings, 106*.

855 Their total of 37 (first innings) at Bournemouth was the season's lowest.

856 K. Day.

857 Bruce Dooland and A. K. Walker.

858 Bryan Lobb.

859 Bill Alley, five for 38 and Bryan Lobb, five for 37.

860 P. B. Wight.

861 J. Harris and G. M. Tripp.

862 Against Hampshire at Bournemouth (match analysis) in July.

863 Brian Statham.

864 Brian Langford, five for 15, J. McMahon, five for 24.

865 J. W. McMahon.

866 He was the first Somerset pace bowler since the war to take 100 wickets in all first-class matches.

867 Henry Horton.

868 T. E. Dickinson from Parramatta, formerly of Lancashire.

869 122 against Worcestershire at Worcester in August 1955.

870 John Langridge and George Cox.

871 27 wickets for 264 runs.

872 M. J. Horton of Worcestershire, his victims being Stephenson, Tremlett and Graham Atkinson.

873 P. Broughton, six for 38 and M. Ryan, four for 32.

874 J. Hilton of Somerset, match figures eight for 69 and M. Hilton of Lancashire, match figures 14 for 88.

875 Denis Brookes.

876 P. B. Wight, 62* and 128* in June 1956.

877 J. Hilton.

878 Bryan Lobb.

THE YEAR 1958

879 The New Zealand captain J. R. Reid.

880 P. B. Wight and Brian Langford.

881 Colin McCool.

882 Against Middlesex at Lord's. Five wickets fell at 147 and the side went from 147 for four to 149 all out.

883 Colin McCool with eight for 74.

884 Peter Wight.

885 Phil Sharpe with 141.

886 Graham Atkinson with 164.

887 J. G. Lomax against Nottinghamshire.

888 Brian Langford.

MORE FROM THE 'FIFTIES ... AND 'SIXTIES

889 D. Slade.

890 Brian Langford, Lancashire, making 89 and 59.

891 Ken Palmer.

892 All were out to David Gibson, unassisted, without scoring.

893 Tom Cartwright.

894 The partnership was worth 316 of which Willie Watson hit 217 and Wharton finished with 120.

895 Tony Lewis and Mike Brearley.

896 W. J. Stewart.

897 Eleven.

898 B. Booth, J. D. Bond and R. Collins.

899 P. R. "Polly" Umrigar who scored 203 in the first Indian innings.

900 Chris Greetham with 104.

901 R. A. Gale with 137.

902 It was his fifth century there.

903 Maurice Tremlett.

904 Peter Wight against Kent.

905 Chris Greetham.

906 Brian Close.

907 Micky Stewart and John Edrich.

908 Peter Wight 106 and Colin McCool 108 against Sussex at Eastbourne.

THE YEAR 1960

909 Atholl McKinnon.

910 It was their first win over Glamorgan in Wales for ten years.

911 E. Bryant.

912 Hugo Yarnold, the former Worcestershire wicket-keeper.

913 W. E. Russell and S. E. Russell.

914 Graham Atkinson and Peter Wight put on 300 for the third wicket.

915 L. C. H. Palairet and C. A. Bernard with 262 v Hampshire at Bournemouth in 1900.

916 He was first in the country to 2000 runs.

917 C. R. M. Atkinson, Abbas Ali Baig and D. R. W. Silk.

918 Harold Gimblett.

THE YEAR 1961

919 D. B. Close.

920 Against Essex at Westcliff when they were all out for 48 in 15.2 overs.

921 The match against Glamorgan at Cardiff.

922 Ken Palmer.

923 Roy Marshall.

924 J. S. Savage who had an innings analysis of six for 72.
925 Ian Bedford who made 52*.
926 Ken Palmer.
927 M. D. Burden who finished with eight for 38.
928 Bill Alley became the first player in the club's history to score two not-out centuries, 183*, 134* in the same match.

THE YEAR 1962

929 Pakistan.
930 Essex at Brentwood.
931 Against Lancashire at Old Trafford where the home side made 74 and 93.
932 Chris Greetham.
933 H. D. "Dicky" Bird.
934 A. R. "Tony" Lewis.
935 Ashby de la Zouch.
936 Colin Atkinson.
937 C. D. Drybrough.
938 Peter Eele.

MORE FROM THE EARLY 1960s

939 Bill Alley with 221* against Warwickshire at Nuneaton.
940 His father, the great West Indian batsman, George Headley, had been professional at Dudley for many years.
941 Dave Halfyard.
942 Tom Cartwright.
943 Four.
944 M. J. Horton 233 and Tom Graveney 164*. Worcestershire made 520 for three.
945 Jimmy Binks.
946 Peter Walker.
947 Roy Virgin, 124, 125* against Warwickshire at Edgbaston.
948 Graham Atkinson who in the second innings made 46* out of 94.

949 Basil Butcher 130 and Garfield Sobers 112.
950 It wasn't played in Derbyshire but in Burton-on-Trent, Staffs.
951 Fred Rumsey.
952 Glamorgan at Neath.
953 A. T. Castell who returned figures of 10 for 102.
954 Ken Palmer.
955 Ken Palmer.
956 D. N. F. Slade.
957 A. Jones of Glamorgan, 187* and 105*.
958 David Doughty.

1964—AN AUSTRALIAN YEAR

959 R. B. Simpson with 125.
960 A. S. Brown, then playing for Gloucestershire.
961 J. R. Gray with 118*.
962 Brian Langford.
963 Sonny Ramadhin.
964 Roy Virgin.
965 J. F. Harvey, 114.
966 Tom Cartwright of Warwickshire.
967 Harold Gimblett, West Indies 1950 (didn't play) and Maurice Tremlett also West Indies 1947-48.
968 Captain and wicket-keeper Harold Stephenson.

THE YEAR 1965

969 G. T. Dowling, 101*.
970 Colin Atkinson. Essex went from 196 for five to 196 all out.
971 Chris Greetham.
972 Ken Palmer.
973 David Larter.
974 Geoff Hall.
975 Wicket-keeper Geoff Clayton, 106.
976 M. G. M. Groves of Oxford University.

977 Chris Greetham.

978 Bill Alley, whose figures were 20–7–34–2 and 26–9–40–6.

1966—THE OTHER WORLD CUP YEAR

979 Conrad Hunte with 206 and Joe Solomon, 104*.

980 Graham Burgess.

981 By Sid Buller.

982 Arthur Jepson.

983 They took part in the first county match to include Sunday play against Essex at Ilford.

984 It was the last day on which first-class cricket was played at Cardiff Arms Park and Somerset were the visitors.

985 Alan Jones had 51 for Glamorgan in the second innings, Bill Alley having made 55 in the Somerset first innings.

986 Against Lancashire at Southport. He put on 145 for the sixth wicket with Ken Palmer.

987 R. Palmer, 6–0-46-0, Bill Alley 12–5–15–2.

988 For the first time ever three bowlers took 100 wickets, Langford, Rumsey and Ken Palmer.

MOSTLY 1966 AGAIN — A BUSY YEAR

989 Fred Rumsey.

990 Mervyn Kitchen, 100.

991 He held a record 42 catches.

992 Brian Langford.

993 P. J. Robinson.

994 David Acfield.

995 Fencing.

996 Mushtaq was his 1000th wicket in first-class cricket.

997 Fred Titmus of Middlesex.

998 Thirteen.

999 John Snow.